JAMES

By Coach Don James

as told to Virgil Parker

JAMES
by Coach Don James
as told to Virgil Parker

COPYRIGHT 1991
by Don James and Virgil Parker

Manufactured in the United State of
America. First edition.

ISBN 0-934904-29-4

Cover design by Win Mumma
Dawgfather poster courtesy of Sports Washington Magazine

Mailing address:
JAMES
6001 South 72nd Street
Lincoln, NE 68516

Contents

chapter one

Was the new coach James from Kent State or Jones from Penn State?

Don James was not exactly a household name in Seattle when I was hired to be the University of Washington's 21st head football coach in 1975.

That point was driven home rather sharply when my wife Carol and I arrived. On our way from the airport to the hotel where we had reservations, we thought it would be fun to drive by the beautiful stadium where I would be working on Saturdays in the fall.

Right out in front of the stadium, in big letters on the marquee, it read:

"WELCOME COACH JONES"

Although some people had obviously never heard of "Coach James", even more seemed to have never heard of Kent State, where I had been the head coach the previous four seasons. But make no mistake. The general reception we received upon our arrival was great. We really felt welcome, even though somewhat unknown in this part of the country.

Carol and me in what serves as my "office" on Saturdays during the fall.

We soon learned that the people in Seattle wanted to know who I was. They probably also wondered why in the world the university had hired a guy from Kent State. At first, everybody thought it was great. They thought I was from Penn State, not Kent State.

Even though I had been one of the top assistants — the defensive coordinator — at such major schools as Florida State, Michigan and Colorado, no one out here had heard of me. That's understandable. You don't get a lot of ink or recognition when you're an assistant.

The whole process of hiring a new coach came about after Jim Owens, who had been at Washington for 18 years, announced early in the 1974 season that it was going to be his last.

Joe Kearney, who is now the commissioner of the WAC Conference, was the Washington athletic director at the time. He started a national search for a new Husky coach. He later told me that his goal was to initially compile a list of about 25 candidates.

Not just 25 names. He wanted men who came well recommended and coaches who had an interest in the job. I heard he called various conference commissioners around the country for recommendations.

Among others, he called Fred Jacoby, who was the Mid-American Conference commissioner — he's now the Southwest Conference commissioner — and Fred recommended Bill Hess of Ohio University and myself. Then Joe Kearney flew around the country, interviewing four or five from each area.

When his plane landed in Cleveland, I knew for a fact that Bill Hess was also a candidate for the job. I saw him in the lobby of the airport hotel while on the way to my interview.

I went through that preliminary interview at the airport hotel with Kearney and Washington assistant athletic director Don Smith, who is still on the staff here.

I had never met Joe before. And we had no more than shaken hands and introduced ourselves than some drunk came up and started badgering us. It was very embarrassing. Apparently this guy recognized me and wouldn't let us go.

Joe said later he was very impressed with the way I diffused the situation. He said he admired the way that I handled the drunk without embarrassing the guy or putting him down. While, at the same time, not letting him cause a scene.

It was a difficult situation. After all, this was a very important moment for me.

You never know what makes a favorable impression on people. Maybe I have the inebriated man to thank for getting the job. In any case, I was selected to come to Seattle for a second interview.

I believe Dan Devine was offered the job and was about ready to take it when he took the Notre Dame job instead. I heard that they were interested in Mike White next and may have offered him the job. At the time Mike was at the University of California.

When Mike decided not to leave Cal, I think it came down to Daryl Rodgers and myself. Rodgers was at San Jose State and had been doing well.

When Carol and I flew out to Seattle for the final interview, it was a long and really rocky flight. We came through a very rough weather front and we were late. They had a dinner and reception all scheduled for us, but the plane was so late we didn't have time to go to the hotel and change.

I have always had a problem with air sickness. I have a private pilot's license, but if it gets real rough I'm going to get sick.

And I was about half sick. If that weren't enough, Joe had to give me the information that my mother had had a heart attack that day. It happened while we were in flight, so Joe had to give me that news on top of everything else.

Then we headed right from the airport to Joe's house for the reception. Some alums were there, along with several university people and a couple of players. Some regents were on hand to meet us. Dr. Flennaugh was one. I also met Vic Markoff, a former player who was a Hall of Famer. I also remember that Dave Cohn, who is now on the board of regents, was there. Mike Reed and Ray Penney were a couple of the players invited to the reception.

Because of the late start, or maybe because they liked us, we were asked to stay over for another day. The next day I had individual meetings with Dr. John Hogness, the university president; Al Ulbrickson, the vice-president in charge of athletics, and many more alums.

I appreciated the way Joe had set up the sessions. I like to interview people the same way. I don't just sit them down and have 10 questions to nail them with. I like to spend time with the person. An evening. Maybe drive around in the car sightseeing, talking about things. I think you can get a pretty good feel of a person that way. It appeared that's what Joe had in mind.

When we left Seattle on Sunday morning, the main headline on the sports page read, "Rodgers to be next head coach."

That's what the media was projecting. I thought I had a good interview, but also had no idea what was going on. It was definitely a job I was interested in. No question about that. I had other interview opportunities, but my wife Carol and I had made up our mind we weren't going to leave Kent State just to get another job. We felt we could stay there and win and enjoy it. We weren't going to leave unless it was a top job, and we surely felt Washington fit that category.

I had always pictured USC as the premiere No. 1 team in the league, followed by UCLA. But some of the coaches I talked to felt Washington could be a challenger. The job is what you make it.

Despite what the paper said, Carol and I felt I was still in the running. In fact we thought we had gained some ground.

Kearney had pretty well told me where he was in the time frame of their decision-making. Since I was the last to be interviewed, I knew an answer would be forthcoming soon.

A couple of days later Joe called and said they'd like to have me. I told him I would have to talk to my athletic director at Kent State (Mike Lude, who later became my A.D. at Washington) before I could make the final decision.

When it came to the contract, they already had a lot of things in force that I felt we needed — a fulltime recruiting coordinator and an academic counsellor. So they had a lot of things already established that I would have wanted assured in a contract. It wasn't a matter of heavy negotiation. Naturally, I wanted to be assured of a full compliment of coaches. I was not that concerned about the length of my contract. The four years I was offered is pretty standard. Most coaches would like to have five. That way an initial recruit is assured you will be his head coach through his career, even if he redshirts.

The program was pretty well laid out. Since they had gone after Dan Devine and Mike White before I was offered the job, they had already developed the package they were going to offer. There was a guest membership to a local country club, the yacht club and the downtown athletic club. And Carol and I were to both receive courtesy cars. The salary wasn't all that much more than I had been making at Kent State. But it was an increase. And there were more options. There was a television show and a radio show. You had the opportunity to create more revenue in a market like Seattle.

But there is always a lot of apprehension in making such a move. You know what you're going to have to go through for the first year or two. I knew it wasn't going to be a lot of fun, but it would be a great challenge.

The first thing you have to face, which I didn't have to do in my first head coaching job at Kent State, is dealing with your existing staff. It just wouldn't work out to take a staff of eight guys with you to a new job. And some wouldn't want to relocate.

And they all had different family situations. The wife of one of my assistants, Fred Gissendaner, had recently died. He was trying to cope as a single parent with two small children. As soon as I got the job I got the staff back there together. Dennis Fitzgerald was named the new Kent State coach. Then he and I decided which assistants he would like to keep and which ones would be invited to come to Seattle with me.

I brought four from Kent State — Skip Hall, Bob Stull, Ray Dorr and Dick Scesniak.

In addition, I wanted to hire a couple of assistants who had not been at Kent State or Washington. One was Jim Mora, who is now the head coach of the New Orleans Saints. Mora and I had been assistants at Colorado together and I had great admiration for his abilities. At the time, Jim was on the UCLA staff.

The other was Chick Harris, who was coaching the Detroit Wheels and had been from Long Beach, California. He's now the running back coach for Chuck Knox with the Seahawks.

Mora was my first key hire. He became my defensive coordinator. Getting Jim really helped in several ways. Not only was he a fine coach, but he was also a good recruiter.

Maybe just as important was the fact that hiring him gave me instant credibility in Seattle. A lot of people were amazed that this guy from Kent State, who nobody had heard of, could hire somebody away from UCLA.

One of the first things I did after being hired was try to reach Mora. But I couldn't find him. In my

Now the head coach of the NFL New Orleans Saints,
Jim Mora was my first defensive coordinator at the
University of Washington.

mind, he was a key. I didn't want to set the rest of the staff until I knew whether Jim would come.

About that time my phone rang. It was Jim calling to congratulate me. And I said, "Where in the world are you? I've been trying to reach you." He told me he was up in the mountains skiing. I told him I wanted him to come to Washington with me.

I heard him turn to his wife and yell, "Connie, we're moving to Washington." And that was it.

Connie was a USC grad. Jim had played at Occidental, however they thought that a move to the Northwest might be good for their family. And this was also a chance for Jim to be a coordinator.

That solved the problem of the Kent State staff and the newcomers I wanted. But then there were Jim Owens' assistants at Washington. I would need to interview them and make some more decisions. Jim Owens had some very qualified assistants and I was able to fit three men into the new staff — Bob Ryan, Ray Jackson and Jim Lambright. And I was very pleased with the adjustment they made.

If there was going to be any problem — and it wasn't one — it would have come from retaining Lambright, who had been Owens' defensive coordinator. But Jim Lambright assured me it would not be a problem to lose that title to Mora.

That turned out to be a great move. Jim Lambright has stayed with me and recruited a lot of the "name" instate prospects for us. And, after Mora left, I moved Lambright back into the role of defensive coordinator. He has since added the title as assistant head coach and has done a great job of coaching and recruiting.

I knew from the outset there would also be the challenge of blending the holdovers, the newcomers and the guys I would bring along from Kent State into a cohesive staff that would pull together as a single unit. But, I honestly didn't feel that was going to be a big issue.

Our coaches arrived in Seattle on the 28th of December. And we went right to work. The signing date for recruits was just around the corner. I wanted to get an airplane and get around the state to see a combination of recruits and alums in the various areas.

That first night, I remember, there was a snowstorm and a basketball game. They had a reception after the game at the hotel where we were staying. The next day we had the whirlwind airplane trip. I visited as many prospects and alums around the state as I could in one day.

I spent the next day in the office interviewing members of the Owens staff. I wanted to complete that as quickly as possible. It was important to their careers to know where they stood and also to get my staff set. There were some who had already made arrangements to do other things. It was a matter of going through the list and giving each coach the opportunity to express himself.

I had information from people who were close to the program and I sat down and spent a lot of time with Coach Owens on the strengths and weaknesses of each assistant. He was very helpful.

When he left coaching, Owens went with a worldwide food service organization. He's since moved into the oil business with Shell. Jim has continued, over the years, to be very interested in the Husky program. He sends clippings about kids he thinks might make a good prospect. He was back for the Centennial game against USC this last season. He was very supportive in getting me started.

One amusing story came out of this business of people wondering who this Don James person was.

I found out later that Jim Cooch, who I coached at Colorado, was living in Seattle. On the day it was announced that I had been named Washington's head coach, Cooch was in the office of Herb Mead, an avid Husky booster.

While he was there, Mead got a phone call from Jim Nordstrom, another influential alum and booster — who later became the owner of the Seattle Seahawks. Nordstrom wanted to know who this James fellow was.

Cooch heard Mead say, "I haveno idea who Don James is."

To which Cooch broke in to say, "He's one of the best coaches in the country." Herb said, "What did you say?" And Jim said, "He was my college coach at Colorado. He is great."

So Herb put Cooch on the phone after telling Nordstrom, "I want you to hear what this guy in my office just said about our new coach."

One other major event during those first few days was my initial press conference in Seattle.

I told the media that we were very capable of winning a conference championship at Washington. Go to the Rose Bowl. Win a Rose Bowl. That we could win a national championship and I could even become the national Coach of the Year. And for those reasons I was interested in the job.

As it turned out, we accomplished four of those five objectives in our third season. The other, the national championship, has eluded us so far.

I also told the media that "we don't dare try to start at the southern most part of the Pac-8 and work our way up. We've got to start at the north, down. For starters, we've got to become a consistently better team than the other Northwest schools. Then, hopefully, we can get better than the Bay Area schools. Then we'll be in a position to attack the two strongest schools (USC and UCLA) in the league."

I added that it would be unrealistic to think we are going to go out and beat USC and UCLA all the time, even though we did beat them both that first year.

I also said we'd have to recruit better in the Northwest to keep our top instate prospects from going to California.

JAMES

For starters, before they went recruiting for the first time, I showed our new coaching staff a USC highlights film so they would know what kind of players it would take for us to reach our goals.

And that's the quality of player our evaluations began to pinpoint and the type of players we began to recruit.

chapter two

*The first order of business
was recruiting. Unlike many
coaches, it's a job I enjoy*

A lot of coaches complain about recruiting. I have never felt that way. I've always enjoyed recruiting. It's a good thing I do, because it is probably the single most important thing we coaches do. I should add that I also look forward to signing day so that we can wrap up another recruiting season.

I enjoy the evaluation process of trying to identify a prospect and I believe that this is by far the most important phase of recruiting. After we go out and look at players, we must identify which of them has the potential to make it. It's a great challenge to look at a 17 or 18-year-old youngster and project whether he is a "can't miss, sure fire prospect" or decide that he is just not going to measure up to the challenge of Division 1 football.

Yet those are the kinds of decisions that keep you in business — or lead to bankruptcy. Much of the time it's not how good a recruiter you are but rather how good an evaluator you are. A staff might look great by

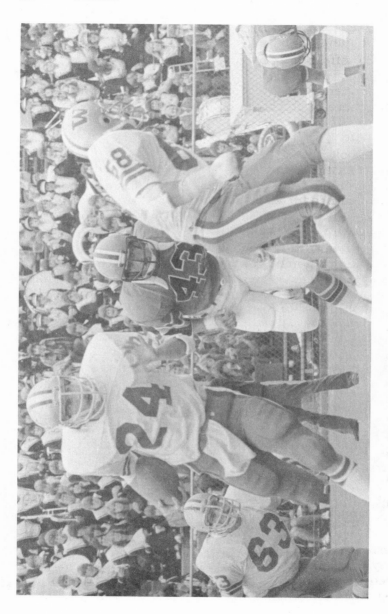

Joe Steele (No. 24), the first top local running back we recruited.

going out and signing 30 guys. But if they can't play, you're going to be history.

So, effective recruiting was a No. 1 priority when we first arrived in Seattle. I wanted us to get the top recruits from the state of Washington and then go out from there. I felt we had to recruit instate to have a chance. If you can't recruit instate, you can't recruit any state.

I took the coaches into a film room before they went recruiting for the first time and showed them a USC film and told them, "That's the kind of players we want and need if we are ever going to win a title."

We got lucky and got some of the top instate kids to come with us at the very beginning. When we first got here we were told the best running back in the state was a junior named Joe Steele. When he came with us the second year along with Roger Westlund, Joe Sanford and some of those kids who were the "name" high school athletes, that really helped us.

In fact, the recruitment of Joe Steele was almost as important to the program as his playing ability later. Here was an athlete we had to have because he would give credibility to our recruiting program.

If Joe had gone off to play in Southern California, two or three of the linemen we were after might have followed. Before you know it, we lose the quarterback we're after. Then you're right back fighting for your life. We might have still gotten where we are today, but it would have taken a lot longer.

That had been one of the complaints about Washington football recruiting before I arrived. The claim was that the Huskies couldn't get the best instate kids.

But suddenly Joe Steele committed and the others started to come in. We were after the top players, but they all had the choice to go to other schools. We needed to break the ice. And the signing of Steele did just that. He was the kind of prospect that you could

Two of our current co-captains came all the way from the State of Virginia to be Huskies.

Don Jones
Outside linebacker
No. 48

Ed Cunningham
Center
No. 79

package up his credentials and get him a scholarship anywhere in the country. Any school!

The battle for instate kids now is mostly between us and Washington State, although the Oregon schools will come up here. Also, Notre Dame works the state some and the California schools will go after a few each year.

The focus of our outstate recruiting has been in California. We recruit the contiguous Pac-10 area, Arizona to Canada. We screen Montana and Idaho, get into Denver a little bit and Hawaii.

Then we do mail order recruiting in the rest of the country. We send out questionnaires to the Blue Chip lists and see if we can scare up any interest. We'll call if there is.

We've found that if there is a family tie in Seattle or the Northwest, then we might have a chance. Very seldom do we get a kid from a long distance away who had zero ties to the state of Washington.

We have two starters from Virginia on our team right now, both of whom will be team captains for the '91 season, who fit in that category. One, Don Jones, has an uncle who is the vice-principal of a school in Bellevue, Washington. The other is Ed Cunningham. His dad worked on the Worlds Fair in Vancouver, B.C., and spent a lot of time out here during the construction stage of the fair.

But back to the challenge of when we first arrived. Mel Thompson, who had been the recruiting coordinator on Jim Owens' staff, had already evaluated the prospects. I don't recall that the previous staff had done a whole lot of recruiting. That usually is not a good use of money to send eight or ten guys on the road who aren't sure they're still going to have a job. You don't get a lot of effective recruiting done that way.

I was interested in the list of prospects who had already been evaluated. We couldn't start all over on the first of January and re-evaluate. We had to go with the list they already had. Michael Jackson, a linebacker from that first group, was from the Tri City area. He played as a freshman and later had a very good career with the Seattle Seahawks.

Nesby Glasgow, who is still playing with the Seahawks as a defensive back, was another of the first-year recruits. It was a good start. Thompson had identified some outstanding prospects.

High school football in the State of Washington is very good. A lot of players in the state will get college scholarships each year, as many as 75 in one year. The average for the Pac-10 is maybe 25 players from Washington each year. In our opinion there are not that many who qualify for our league, but other schools will take them.

And it's interesting. If we recruit 12 and another 13 who we didn't even recruit go elsewhere in the conference, there will be a couple of those who will pan out to be pretty darn good.

I enjoy going into the homes of the prospects. And I've been in hundreds and hundreds of homes over the years. Generally, it's an enjoyable experience, although there have been some difficult visits.

I've dealt with the finest parents you could ever want to meet. And alcoholic parents who weren't so great to deal with. I've been through it all. But it's fun to go into a home and talk to parents about their son's future. They are so concerned about him and so proud of him. It gets a little easier as you have gained a bigger name in the field of coaching and people know who you are before you arrive. And when the team has had success, that also helps. The quality of the school that you represent means a lot.

The most memorable home visit I ever had came a couple of years ago when we were recruiting a running back in Los Angeles named Beno Bryant. He lived in an area of LA where you had to be a little careful after dark.

It turned out to be an exciting evening when Coach Slade
and I visited the home of Beno Bryant.

Coach Larry Slade and I were talking to the boy's parents when we suddenly heard gun shots right next door. The houses were so close together it was just like it was coming from the next room.

Larry asked the father, "Shall we hit the floor?" After all, we weren't accustomed to sitting in someone's living room and hearing gun fire, but the dad said, "Unless it's a Uzi (an automatic weapon) we don't worry about it."

As sirens blared just outside, we went ahead with our visit. When we got ready to leave, an ambulance and the police were next door. When we came out of the house there was a helicopter overhead with the lights shining down on all of us in the area. Needless to say, Larry and I sprinted to the car and took off.

We read in the paper the next day that Todd Bridges, who was one of the stars on the TV series "Different Strokes" had been involved. He was the older kid on the series with Gary Coleman. According to the papers, some dispute arose over a drug transaction. Bridges was arrested but released for cocaine possession and, after a retrial, was acquitted of attempted murder and manslaughter charges after the shooting of an accused drug dealer in a crack house.

In another incident in California, a recruit was trying to avoid all coaches on signing day because he couldn't make up his mind where he was going. When I pulled up in front of his house to sign him, he came running out, jumped in his car and took off. And I was right behind. It was like a cops and robbers high speed chase. I followed him all over the hills of San Pedro. He finally stopped at a house and got out of his car. I didn't know where we were. It turned out we were in front of his high school coach's house and he wanted to change his mind.

He told me that he didn't think he wanted to go to the University of Washington. I started asking him why, basically re-starting the recruiting process all over again. He admitted that another school had gotten ahold of him the night before and turned him around. I covered a few things in comparison to the other school. I wasn't negative about them but just pointed out the advantages of Washington on each point.

I talked about the size of the two schools, the prestige of the schools, the academic image of the school, the stadium size, the league — the other school was not in the Pac-10 —and asked him how he would rate the two schools on those five things.

"Well,' he said, "I'd have to rate the University of Washington first on all those points." So, I asked him what he was going to do. And he said, "Well, now I'm not sure."

I told him it sounded like he opened the door to some recruiting the night before and wound up confused. I suggested we go in and talk to his coach. We spent quite some time. I found out that the other college coach was coming over there to sign him. So, obviously, the whole thing had been worked out with the high school coach.

I was a little outnumbered. We talked and talked. I just said enough to turn him back to our side. We spent another hour, and I could see that they had told this other coach that he wouldn't sign with us.

So I said, "How much time do you want? An hour? Two hours? You just tell me and I'll leave and come back to get this paper signed later on."

That's what I did. But when I got back, the other coach was still there. But the prospect finally did sign with us.

It can sometimes get to be a tug-of-war right down to the final gun. In fact, in that case, the recruiting 'game' went into about a four-hour overtime.

Another interesting case occurred when we were recruiting Phil Carter, a running back from Tacoma. He eventually went to Notre Dame. Anyway, one evening a booster called our home. I was in California, but he told Carol that she should go down to see Phil and make sure he was going to be a Husky.

Although she often went with me and has always been a great help with recruiting, she said she wasn't going to do anything unless I called and told her to do so. The booster found me by phone, then called Carol back and said he had talked to me and that I had said it was okay.

He picked her up about nine at night and they went to Carter's house. They tried to sell the Huskies and why he should stay at home. By now it was 11 p.m. His folks said that a prayer meeting would help with such a big decision. So everybody got in a car and went to their minister's house.

Carol said the place was filled with people. By this time it's midnight. Everybody was standing around holding hands and praying. The booster turned to Carol and said, "We're in trouble. He's going to go to Notre Dame."

They left, went home and called me. They said that after an hour-long prayer meeting they were sure he was going to Notre Dame. And he did.

Then there was the case of Tom Erlandson. We had gotten a call about a kid in Denver. We suggested they send some film. At that time, Ray Dorr was recruiting Denver for us.

The film came, but Ray was leaving to be interviewed for the head coaching job at Southern Illinois, so he just stuck the film in his desk, intending to look at it when he returned. When Ray went for his interview, things worked out real well, they liked him and hired him.

Ray called from Illinois and said they had offered him the job. He wanted to know if he could just stay there and get started with his new job. I congratulated him and said, "Ray, it's all right with me. You're not on my staff any more. You can stay as long as you want."

Well, the film on the Denver prospect just sat in Ray's desk. We didn't even know we had it. As it turned out, Tom Erlandson's dad had played pro ball at San Diego with Chuck Allen, who had been a great player for the Huskies. Chuck now works in personnel with the Seahawks. It was Chuck who actually got the film over to Dorr.

Chuck called and wanted to know if we had made a decision on Erlandson. He said the parents would like to know and get the film back. That's when I found out that Tom Erlandson's godfather was Marv Harshman, who was the Washington basketball coach.

Marv had been the basketball coach at WSU when Tom's dad —Tom, Sr. — had played his college ball. The father had said many times when his son was growing up that he wished he'd had the chance to play for the Huskies.

That prompted the boy's mother to say she was going to make sure her son was evaluated by us so he wouldn't go through life saying he should have played for Washington.

Well, we went through Ray's desk and found the film on this linebacker from Denver. I gave it to Jim Lambright, our defensive coordinator. I remember him saying, "I hope this guy is not a prospect." He said that because it was late. It was toward the end of January. And our list of top prospects was pretty well set.

We looked at the film and this young Tom could run and he was tough. Then we found out he was also Marv Harshman's godson and that his dad played pro ball. So we jumped on him. Gary Pinkel made a quick trip to Denver and later I made a trip. We met his parents and talked with them at the Stapleton Airport in Denver. Then we flew him in for a quick visit. We swooped in at the end and got him. He had quite a few choices. The University of Colorado was really after him.

He was a good player for us. When it comes to recruiting, you never know.

If there is anything about the recruiting process I dislike it's what can develop later on — the job of coaching bad kids. Youngsters with a character problem that slip through the cracks.

Through our evaluation process we try to avoid that kind of person. But the system is not perfect. When you wind up with a problem player on your campus, the easiest way to solve the problem would be to kick the kid off the team. But of course, that's not the way to go. You're obligated to help the youngster if you can. The first step is counseling. Over the years, we have tried to change attitudes. No matter what it is, whether it's getting him into the classroom, getting him to stop doing something that is harmful or correcting his social problems, we try to teach them to be responsible citizens.

If a player makes any mistakes, you get involved. The ones who make life tough for a coach are the ones who will not change. They eventually force you into eliminating them, and that's always traumatic.

Fortunately, that hasn't involved very many players, but there will always be some, and it doesn't take very many to disrupt things. It's a painful thing because you have to become a detective. You have to get the facts. Then you have to be the judge.

You've heard the accusations. You've talked to the player. Now you have to sit in judgement. And that's not a lot of fun. After all, you impact the player's life with your decision — maybe for years and years to come.

I've gotten to the place with a few players where all the work and counseling was to no avail. Then the only thing you can do that might change them, might straighten out their lives, is to fire them.

We've dropped young men who then went to other schools, straightened out and turned into good citizens.

Yet I don't think they would have here. They were just going to see how long they could test us. The fact that we dropped them from the team may have shocked them back into reality. They say to themselves, "Coach told me not to do this. Coach told me this was wrong. I didn't correct myself so now I'm done. I'm out of business."

I've had them come back crawling and in tears. And the parents come in, too. That's why, whenever we put a player on any kind of probation, we put it in writing and send a copy to the parents.

The challenge of recruiting is that something needs rebuilding every year — offensive backs, defensive line, receivers, defensive backs.

But one of the real challenges of college coaching is the fact that we have a 25-30 percent turnover every year. After each season we have to recruit to fill the holes, followed by our winter conditioning program and then spring practice. That's the fun of coaching. You get to coach and teach and watch the men improve, but you don't have to play a game every week of the year.

The pressure of our year is the season, the bowl game and recruiting. The rest of our year is still a lot of fun for me. We get to go about what we are doing without the pressure of having to win a game each and every Saturday.

I wouldn't expect anybody to believe that major college football saves every kid that came out of the ghetto. But, by the same token, it has offered an opportunity for a lot of young people. If they paid attention, I think that a lot of coaches — and hopefully I'm one of them — gave those youngsters a lot of good advice while they were in the program.

The lessons of preparing for a game — competing, playing hard and being team players while learning to play by the rules — can also be applied to preparation for life after football.

That's one of the key things. The ability to be goal-oriented, but to place team goals ahead of personal goals. Such an attitude will obviously be valuable to them when they join some business later in their careers. And there are lessons in courage to be learned. And persistence. I could name many, many more.

I get a lot of letters from former players. Many of them have written, "I learned more in your program than I learned up on the hill in class."

There are a lot of things of value that can be learned from football on how to deal with problems, on how to work hard and compete. We have some ideas that we talk to our players about that are in our playbook — the ingredients of being a good team player. We define the ingredients and talk a lot about them.

No. 1 is giving 100 percent. No. 2 is having courage on and off the field. They probably have to make more courageous decisions off the field in their choices about life. No. 3 is mental. How to master your position and not hurt your organization with mental mistakes. If a player makes a mistake, we want it to be a physical mistake from going all out, not a mental mistake.

No. 4 is the matter of caring. The ability to put the team ahead of personal goals. Successful organizations have a lot of people who are caught up in the team concept.

No. 5 is loyalty. I remind them that there is seldom a problem with loyalty until there is adversity. I want them to stand up for their teammates when someone outside the team says something derogatory about a coach or player. At the same time, within the team, there should be no sniping. If they've got a problem, they should come to the coaches and talk it out.

Those are lessons, and I think valuable lessons, which will serve them well on a business team or any other team for the rest of their lives.

chapter three

*The first two years
at Washington were
extremely difficult*

It's no wonder Jim Owens decided that 1974 was going to be his last year as the coach of the Huskies. For my first season in '75 I inherited a very difficult schedule.

We had to open up at Arizona State. And Frank Kush had a great team down in Tempe. Later that year the Sun Devils won the Fiesta Bowl by beating Nebraska and finished with a perfect 12-0 record.

Second on the schedule was a fine Texas team. Although we weren't blown out of either game — we lost the opener 12-35 and to the Longhorns, 10-28 — we were quickly 0-2.

We managed to even up our record with wins over Navy and Oregon, but then we had to go on the road to Alabama. And Bear Bryant beat us 52-0.

After that lopsided loss to Alabama I moved into my office. I mean literally. I took my pajamas and a toothbrush and lived in my office from Sunday until Wednesday of each week the rest of the season.

We had a new staff and a new team. I had to send a message. There were a lot of seniors, in fact we were top heavy with seniors. I felt I had to send a message that said, "I'm not about to give up on this season and I don't want any of you to do so."

I would recommend that to anybody who is in a position of authority in any job. You can scream and holler at people, but that isn't necessarily going to change things. But if they see how serious and dedicated you are, they are likely to do their best to follow suit.

Things didn't turn around immediately. We dropped a tough three-point decision to Stanford, 24-21, but then bounced back to win four of our final five games of the season.

In the process we really surprised a lot of folks by beating both USC and UCLA. In our final game of the year we edged Washington State which gave us a perfect record against the other three Northwest schools.

Back to that three-point loss to Stanford at home. If we hadn't missed one of the extra points we would have trailed by just two and could have kicked a field goal for a win. Toward the end of the game we were down close but felt we had to go for a touchdown for a victory.

Our only loss in those last five games came when we went down to play Cal in Berkeley and dropped a narrow 27-24 decision.

Danny Lloyd intercepted a pass in the fourth quarter and ran it almost all the way back when we were just three points down. If we had beaten Stanford, we could have kicked a field goal for a tie against Cal and gone to the Rose Bowl. That's how close we were that very first year, despite the terrible start.

So we finished that first year with a 6-5 record. I don't think people were too upset. After all, Washington didn't have a winning season either of the two years prior to my coming. That, plus the fact that we had beaten both USC and UCLA.

Warren 'Harold' Moon with the Husky mascot.

The only losing season I've had came the next year. All those seniors had departed and we were playing a lot of new guys. We wound up 5 and 6.

I think most people accepted the fact that my second season was going to be a rebuilding situation.

That's when Warren Moon became our starting quarterback. His name was Harold Moon when we recruited him. He changed it to Warren when he came to Seattle.

The media wrote a lot about whether or not Warren should be the quarterback, but I didn't think it was causing a split among the players. The media always makes more out of it than the coaches and players do.

We try to look at right guard the same as left guard. And right tackle the same as quarterback. It's just two guys competing for a job. You let them compete and then — regardless of how they have played in the past — you start the one who is doing the best job at the moment.

We have had a lot of starters over the years who have lost their job. It's not an easy thing for a coach to do. We were probably more careful that year, since we were a relatively new staff. We wanted to be fair and give everybody an opportunity to prove themselves.

Chris Rowland had been the starter the year before, although we had recruited Moon out of a junior college our first spring. He showed up the next fall and saw quite a bit of action my first season. He then became the starter in our second season and also for our third which was climaxed by that great Rose Bowl victory over Michigan.

Many fans, the media and maybe some coaches are guilty of thinking the win-loss record reflects the ability of the quarterback.

When things weren't going as well as we would have liked, I always said that Warren Moon doesn't play defense. Warren Moon can't help it if the receiver drops the ball or doesn't get open. Or if a runner fum-

bles. All of those things affect an offense and the outcome of games, but are things over which the
quarterback has no control.

So, after two seasons, we were 6 and 5 and then 5
and 6. And, according to some, it was all Warren
Moon's fault. As a coach I couldn't buy that.

Some people also tried to make the situation at
quarterback a black-white issue. Some would have you
believe that Moon was booed because he was black.
When that was happening, the thing we tried to empha-
size to Warren was that if you're a quarterback, it
doesn't matter what color you are. If you don't move
the ball and don't win, you're going to get booed. But
we stuck with him.

Even when he was booed, Warren held his head
high. And he worked to get better to help the team. I
respect him for the way he handled it.

Later, in a game against USC, he went back to pass,
but nobody was open. So he ran 70-some yards for a
touchdown. The whole stadium was going, "Moon,
Moon." At first I thought they were still booing him.
But the fans had finally changed from "boo" to "Moon".

Warren grew up in a house full of girls. He had
five sisters. He was a very polite and fine young man.
He had only gone to junior college one year. Chick Harris, our LA recruiter, told me he had a quarterback who
was only a freshman but that he wanted to come out.

There was no way we'd recruit him. The junior college coaches would not appreciate you recruiting one of
their players who still had a year of eligibility remaining. I told Chick that Moon's coach would have to give
us approval that it would be okay to recruit him. And
Warren's coach approved the idea of letting him come
out to a major college after just one year.

We liked what we saw of Warren. He threw the
ball a lot at the junior college. And we liked him when
he got here. He had a strong arm and was a good
worker. I think that's one of the reasons he's been so

durable in Canada and the NFL with the Houston Oilers. I know he's the strongest of any quarterback I've ever coached.

Warren showed even more improvement his senior year. But the team was improved as well.

chapter four

The third season turnaround!
A great Rose Bowl victory
after a one-win, three-loss start

A month into our third season it would have taken a person even more optimistic than me to predict a Pac-10 championship and a Rose Bowl victory.

After two years with 6-5 and 5-6 records, we won just one of our first four games at the start of the third season.

It didn't help that we lost our opener to Mississippi State at home, although we then beat San Jose State. Next, we went on the road for two games and lost both of them in the last few seconds after being ahead.

At Syracuse, where I wasn't all that thrilled with the officiating, we were edged 22-20 when they kicked a field goal with just five seconds left in the game.

We went to Minnesota the next week and had a good lead until a bunch of offensive linemen got hurt. After that, we couldn't move the ball at all and we were just trying to hang on. But Minnesota scored with 32 seconds left to beat us 19-17.

The fact that those were both close, two-point losses didn't help. They were still losses.

So, it was crunch time and a difficult time for all of us. A lot of pressure along with a lot of negative stuff from the media, students, and the fans. We just felt like we had to circle the wagons as a team. We talked about it. We knew we were better than this and it was time to prove it. We had to get strength from within and not get caught up in all the outside business and play our game.

It was also a critical time for me — the start of the third year of a four-year contract. And, when you have an overall record of 12 wins and 14 defeats you tend to get a little nervous. Besides, we were getting ready to start league play.

Our first game was at Oregon. The distance from Seattle to Eugene isn't all that great so in those days we traveled down there by bus. I learned early in my career that when you put a team on a couple of buses, the kids want to race. You know, "Let's pass and beat that guy." You don't want a football team, the day before a game, worrying about racing buses, or getting in front or being first. The way I always worked it, I would designate which bus would lead and the players were assigned to bus No. 1 or bus No. 2. Then you've got control over what's going on.

First bus, second bus. And that's the way they'd stay. We always instructed the bus drivers on this. And they knew exactly where we would stop to eat and stop to stretch. The whole itinerary of the trip was planned in advance. And the bus drivers knew it.

Well, we're just down below Olympia. I had been reading and wasn't paying attention when I looked up and saw this bus running along ahead of us. I said to one of the assistants, "Is that our bus up there." He said it was. I was sitting in the first row, so I leaned forward and told our driver, "We're the first bus and we need to get up in front." But he wouldn't do it. He wouldn't go around.

I don't know how many miles it was, 30, 40, 50. I just kept getting madder and madder. I didn't want to make a scene in front of the players, but we had a policy and we're paying the bill and the driver is damn well going to drive the bus the way we tell him to — as long as we don't ask him to break any laws.

So, when we stopped for lunch, I ripped into him. I told him the request was not unreasonable, especially since he was told before we started what the order was to be. I told him I couldn't do anything about it now, but that he sure wasn't going to drive us back. Well, before we ever got to Eugene, he pulled into the bus station in Portland and we changed bus drivers there.

It became a real big deal with the media. "James fires bus driver." It may have not been that big a thing, but when you're 1 and 3 and starting league play, the pressure was beginning to mount. I just didn't need another irritation.

At the start of every season I have each player make out a list of goals. I do the same. The Sunday night before that Oregon game, realizing that I was not meeting my goals and that I was in the third year of a four-year contract and could be history if we played seven more games the way we had the first four, I tore up my "goal sheet".

I wrote two things down on a card: "Thick skin" and "Get it going."

"Thick skin" was to remind me that I was spending too much time worrying about what everybody was saying — the press and the fans. All the sniping. I was even having alums stopping by the office. I wasn't going to spend any more time worrying about that. Just get it going.

I also asked the players to re-write their goals with one thought in mind. "What can I do to help this team today." I told them, "We're going to forget all that nifty goal-setting and just focus on what you can do to help the team THIS week."

I told them to stop thinking that Spider Gaines or Warren Moon will do it. Instead, it had to be an attitude that "I will do it."

And the team had a great game against Oregon. We scored 54 points and could have scored more. Shut them out, 54-0. We had 474 yards in total offense and held them to just 97.

This was a game we went in as the underdogs. Oregon was favored.

We may have only been 2-3, but at least we were undefeated in league play. It was a start, even though we could still end up two and nine. So we were a long way from being out of the woods.

If fact, the media and the fans remained skeptical. They were going to wait and see how we did against the big boys from down south.

In any case, the bus trip home from Oregon was much better. And it goes without saying that with our new driver, our No. 1 bus led the way.

Stanford at home was next. We were ahead 17-0 when they scored twice to catch up to 17-14. But we scored four touchdowns in the fourth quarter that counted and one more that was called back to win it, 45-21. It was one of the greatest fourth quarters I've ever seen.

There were two great things about that game. One was that we answered the challenge when they closed the gap to 17-14. The other was the change in attitude that had come over our players. When Stanford scored those two touchdowns, and I looked up and down the bench, the players had a "Let's get it going!" attitude, not one of despair. I think that helped give us some confidence for the rest of the season.

And that's the way they were the remainder of the season after that bad start. You'd see guys get up from one block and head down field to make another. They were going the extra mile.

After Stanford, Oregon State came to Seattle for what turned out to be an unexpectedly close game. In fact they led 3-0 at halftime. We didn't generate much offense that day. But we got a couple of touchdowns and they only managed one more field goal in the fourth quarter and the final was Washington 14, Oregon State 6.

That made us 3-0 in league play and we were beginning to pick up a few fans. But we were looking at three games in a row coming up against the other California schools and two of the three were going to be on the road.

First we had UCLA. It was 6-6 at halftime, but we lost it 20-12. After the season, however, that game was turned into a victory because they, like Mississippi State, used an ineligible player against us.

The next week we were in Berkeley to play Cal. It was an amazing first half. California led 21-17 after just 15 minutes of play. They had the run and shoot offense.

But we came back and really got after them in the second half, scoring 33 points. That was a good comeback. We were down at halftime, yet made the adjustments and did a good job.

That brought us to the USC game in LA. We led 7-3 at halftime and went to 21-3 before winning it, 28-10.

By this time we were in great shape with the fans. Any time you could beat USC, that was over and above what the fans expected.

The final regular season game was against Washington State. We scored the first three times we had the ball to go up 21-0 in the first quarter. We added touchdowns in the second and third quarters to make it 35-0. WSU scored 15 points in the fourth quarter, but we won it, 35-15.

We had completed the regular season with just the one loss in league play to UCLA. But UCLA had also

Carol lets out a yell — while I'm pretending to remain calm — as a USC field goal beats UCLA and puts us in the 1978 Rose Bowl.

lost once, to Stanford, and still had USC to play. We had a bowl bid tied in. If UCLA went to the Rose Bowl, we would go to the Bluebonnet Bowl.

Well, USC beat 'em, 29-27, when Frank Jordan kicked a field goal on the last play of the game.

The game was on TV. We had sets all around our house. We had decided we were going to have a few close friends in to watch the game with us.

But the media decided they wanted to be at our house, too. So the newspaper sportswriters who covered us and the TV guys with their camera crews all came over and set up.

They had microwave discs and the whole thing out in our driveway. As it turned out, athletic director Mike Lude, his wife Rena, our daughter Jill and Her husband Jeff and our daughter Jeni were on hand. With all the media, we didn't have room for any more close friends.

It was pretty much a tossup game. Obviously we were pulling for USC.

There were a lot of scores, so we had a lot of ups and downs, highs and lows during the game. USC would get ahead and we'd be jumping up and down. Then UCLA would get ahead and we'd sit there down in the dumps. My brother Art called at halftime when USC was ahead. "You're on your way to the Rose Bowl," he said. I warned him, "It's not over yet."

And, sure enough, it wasn't. UCLA got ahead in the second half. But USC got down close as time was running out. But the Trojans didn't have any more time outs. Their field goal team came running on the field full speed. They quickly lined up and kicked the field goal with two seconds showing on the clock. The ball sailed through the uprights as time ran out.

To steal the line, there was a lot of joy in Mudville. There was a lot of screaming and hollering during USC's last drive to get down close. I know the TV cameras had a lot of shots of us coming out of our chairs.

Somebody came to the door the minute the game ended and from then on the front door never got closed. People were streaming in and out. The house just filled up. There were people in our living room I don't think I'd ever seen before.

The neighborhood kids lined our driveway. They were banging on the bottom of pans they had taken from their mother's kitchen. They formed a kind of reception line.

I didn't see much of that because I was on the phone the rest of the night. Friends, family, coaches I'd worked with in the past. They were all calling. That was an exciting evening.

Washington hadn't been to a bowl game for the previous 13 seasons. The Huskies, under Jim Owens, played Illinois in the Rose Bowl following the 1963 season, losing 17-7.

I think people were pretty excited and proud of what we had accomplished. It was some turnaround, from 6-5 and 5-6 my first two seasons and a 1-3 start that year to league champion — and eventually, Rose Bowl winners!

chapter five

The James Gang:
Four boys born to
Thomas and Florence

I was born on New Year's Eve, an hour before midnight. I'm told the doctor who delivered me was dressed in a tuxedo, having been summoned from a party.

The birth took place in our "home" — which was a double garage with no indoor toilet facility.

On December 31, 1932, not very many people in Massillon, Ohio — or anywhere else in the country for that matter — owned a tuxedo. Nor were they going to a party to celebrate the New Year. It was expected that 1933 was going to be a tougher year than '32. The country was in the dark days of the Great Depression.

The garage in which I was born served as a "temporary" home for our family until my father, Thomas, was able to complete a house on the same property in December of 1941.

Although my mother, Florence, attended high school, my dad had to quit school and go to work after the sixth grade.

Thomas and Florence James. Taken shortly before World War II.

My father was extremely hard working. He worked two jobs — in the steel mill and as a bricklayer — to provide the money for four boys to get to college. He and my mother were very education conscious. My three brothers and I all went through college. That was my parent's goal, to see that we got the education they never received.

Dad worked from midnight until 8 o'clock in the morning at the steel mill, then he'd go lay brick for eight hours, sleep for four hours and then go do it all over again. Five straight days every week!

The only time he got a rest was when he would be moved to a day shift at the Republic Steel Mill and thus couldn't work the second job.

It took my parents nearly 16 years to assemble the original James Gang.

My oldest brother Tommy was born in 1924. I also had a brother named Jimmy who I never knew. He was killed before I was born after being hit by a car.

Art was born eight years after Tommy and 18 months before me. John is the youngest. He was born in 1939.

A short time after World War II began, Tommy joined the service.

Art and I — he still lives in Massillon right next door to our original house — were real close and had a sibling rivalry. We split the chores after Tommy went into the service, always arguing over whose turn it was to mow the lawn.

Tommy played for Paul Brown at Massillon High and at Ohio State. After the war he played for the Detroit Lions for a year, then seven or eight more with the Cleveland Browns. Otto Graham was their quarterback. Tommy was a defensive back and he also held the ball on PATs and field goals for Lou Groza. Then he had his last year with the Baltimore Colts.

Tommy is retired now. He was a sales representative for a trucking firm after he finished his pro football

The James boys in 1979. From the left: John, me, Art and Tommy.

Tommy, Jr., holds brother John. Art is on the left.
That's me in the middle.

career. He stayed in Massillon. The firm he worked for was headquartered in Akron.

Art was a class ahead of me in school. He is actually about a year and a half older. He went to Heidelberg College. He worked his whole career with Goodyear Aerospace. He is now retired.

My youngest brother John is in television in Syracuse, N.Y. Among other things, he produces and directs the Syracuse University football and basketball coach's shows.

Like Art, John also played college ball at Heidelberg. Art was a tackle and John was a quarterback. They both had good small college football careers.

I don't remember going out to play ball with my dad in the yard when I was young, but my parents were always at my games.

There was one year that my younger brother John was playing Thursday nights on the junior high school team, I was playing Friday nights, Art was playing Saturday at Heidelberg and Tommy was playing Sunday with the Browns. And our parents would get to all four games if the Browns were at home in Cleveland.

Mom and dad couldn't follow me near as much when I got to college because I was so far away at Miami. But they were very supportive and good parents.

In those days, the bucks were tough to come by. We were not what you'd call real poor. At least we never thought we were poor. We didn't know of anything different.

I guess because of my dad, I developed a strong work ethic. I started working for my uncle's construction company during the summers, carrying bricks when I was nine years old. That hard work helped shape my future, however, because I told myself there had to be an easier way to make a living. I became determined to go to college and not work in construction the rest of my life.

At age eight in 1940.

Somebody must have thought up the 'James Gang' theme when I was just three years old.

I liked fishing better than golf when I was four years old.

At the start of each summer my arms would be dead tired. I'd just go home, take a shower and go to sleep. I remember when cement blocks were invented. Brick layers walked off the job. They said "those things will never work. Nobody will be crazy enough to lift those heavy things all day long." Obviously, they were wrong.

I can remember straddling the rafters and building a chimney. They'd pitch the bricks up through the rafters. I'd catch them and put them in place.

I worked at that every summer until the year between my junior and senior years in college. I had to go to an ROTC camp that year and couldn't work. I'm not sure which experience was the toughest.

Before I was born, my parents had bought this lot. On the back of it they built the double garage in which I was born. It had a kitchen, a living room and a bedroom.

I can remember seeing the foundation being dug for our house in front of the garage. But it was a long time before that became a reality.

Mom's three brothers were all bricklayers. So we'd build each others houses. We'd get sandstone, cut it and lay it. We'd all do the carpentry work.

As I said, my brother Art's house is right next door. It's sandstone. My uncle, Dwayne Haines, was just two blocks around the corner. Any time anybody in the family built a house we'd all chip in and do the work evenings and weekends until it was finished.

My dad died a couple of days before a game against Toledo my first year as the head coach at Kent State in 1971. My mom passed away in 1975, the week of the UCLA game my first year out here at Washington.

I'll deal with the trauma of their deaths, and a couple of other immediate family near tragedies that we have suffered through, later in the book.

chapter six

Started going steady at 14;
Married when we were 19;
And we're still best friends

My wife Carol and I first met when we were 14 years old. It was the summer after our ninth grade, just before we started in high school as sophomores.

I lived just outside of Massillon. Her house was three or four miles away toward Canton. The two towns were eight miles apart.

In that part of Ohio they had what they called "Firemen's Festivals". It was a carnival-like event to raise money to support the local volunteer fire department.

Carol was there with a girl friend. I was with a friend of mine named Jim Bowers. I didn't know either of the girls, but Jim did and introduced me to them.

Carol has told lots of people that she took a liking to me right away, but she also claims I was more attracted to her girl friend than her. I'm smart enough, however, to have denied that all these years.

As I recall, I did walk her girl friend home that night. But the next night I went over to Carol's house

With Carol on her 16th birthday.

Carol's parents, Wayne and Velma Hoobler.

to see her. She also claims I did that because I found out her father had a pool table and a ping pong table in their rec room.

In a way, it was athletics that drew Carol and me together. She was quite a sprinter. In fact she claimed nobody her age could beat her, including any boy in town. It's too bad they didn't have more in the way of organized sports for girls in those days. Carol would have excelled.

A few weeks later Jim and I went over to Carol's house. She was beating us both at pool and ping pong. That's when Jim said, "Carol, I think I finally found someone who can beat you at running." She looked at me and said, "No way."

Well, I won the race. And she says that's what won her heart.

But it was a long distance romance for the first year. Carol only lived in Ohio in the summertime. She went to school and lived in Florida in the winters. We had only known each other for a couple of months when it was time for her to go back down south.

The next summer, before our junior year, Carol told her folks she wanted to stay in Ohio. She enrolled in Lincoln High School in Canton, which was the closest to her home.

Neither of us lived in the actual township limits of Massillon or Canton. In those days, the kids who lived somewhere between the two towns could choose whichever school they wanted in either direction.

In the spring of our junior year — we must have turned 16 by then because I know Carol was driving — during the lunch hour at her school she drove over to Massillon and enrolled for her senior year.

Her parents, Wayne and Velma Hoobler, didn't know anything about it until a few weeks later. That's when her folks got a phone call from Massillon High, checking to make sure where Carol lived and whether or not she was eligible to go to school there.

Carol and me at the high school's "Sweet Sixteen" festivities.

But her mom and dad didn't really mind and that's how we wound up together for our senior year and graduated from high school in the same ceremony.

Hoobler was Carol's maiden name. That's German. She has two sisters, Vietta and Donna Faye. I'm Welsh-Irish. Anyway, when we were considering colleges, Carol at first thought she would go to Capitol University, a Lutheran college in Columbus, Ohio, if I stayed in the state.

But she had a health problem and was advised that she should go south. She had psoriasis and needed to be in a warm, sunny climate. So she decided on the University of Miami. Luckily, as I'll discuss later, I got a scholarship to Miami so we were able to stay in school together.

Carol and I were married after our sophomore year, so we were married the two years I was Miami's starting quarterback. And she was a cheerleader.

In fact, at the end of her sophomore year, just before we got married, the varsity lettermen at the University of Maimi chose Carol as the 'M' Club sweetheart.

During our junior year she went to all the athletic events and banquets as the representative of the 'M' Club.

Carol and I married on August 9, 1952, the summer between our sophomore and junior years in college. We moved out of our dorm rooms and into married student housing right across the street.

We managed financially okay because I was on scholarship and her parents said they would continue to send Carol the same money they had before for her tuition and the cost of room and board in the dorm, with the stipulation that she stay in school and get her degree. I wouldn't have let her quit anyway, so it worked out very well.

There weren't very many married players back then. Our senior year, I think we were the only couple.

A New Year's Eve dance in 1948

It was easier being married because we didn't have to worry about dating. Many evenings we stayed home and studied rather than going out on dates. It was really the best thing we could have done. We settled down and put a lot more emphasis on our school work.

So we started going steady as 14-year-olds and married when we were 19. And nearly 40 years later we're still enjoying each other. I don't suppose that's exactly the norm any more.

So, besides graduating from high school together, we both completed our degrees and graduated together after four years of college. And that's not exactly the norm for an athlete any more either.

chapter seven

Massillon, Ohio, is
a great supporter
of high school sports

If ever there was a football town, Massillon, Ohio
was it. It has always gone all out to support its high
school teams. When I was playing there, you'd walk
downtown and see your picture in the store windows.

Some people have accused Massillon and other
towns in that area of eastern Ohio and western Pennsylvania — Massillon is 50 miles south of Cleveland and
90 miles west of Pittsburgh — of overemphasizing prep
sports.

But from the time I was very young I grew up in
the system, so I didn't know anything different. In
Massillon it was football the year around. If, after the
season, you didn't go out for basketball you went into a
winter football program. If you weren't out for baseball
or track in the spring you had spring football.

Even in the summertime we would meet and run
plays. I don't know if that was legal or not, but we did
it and so did the teams we played. I thought that was
the way it was supposed to be. We had so much success

The quarterback of two Massillon High state
championship teams.

I thought that was the way it was everywhere in the country.

Our graduating class had four or five hundred kids, so it was a pretty good sized school, and our section of the state had all the top teams.

Now, Cincinnati Moeller has kind of taken over as the king-pin of high school football in Ohio.

There were no state championship playoffs in those days. A mythical state champion was chosen. And we were state champs both years when I was a junior and a senior.

My junior year I started on defense and was a backup quarterback. As a senior I was the first string quarterback and we won the state championship in my last game. We played Canton McKinley.

That was an exciting game, and I was as fired up as I have ever been. Canton was rated No. 1. We were No. 2. The winner was going to be the state champion. We won it 6-0.

One thing about that game I'll never forget. We weren't a team to audible or change plays at the line of scrimmage. But Coach Mather told me that Canton McKinley had a defense they almost always used in short yardage situations. It was a seven diamond. When they were in that, they had no way of covering our tight ends. And we were a two tight end team in those situations.

So we worked out an audible system. If I saw the seven diamond defense, I was to yell to the tackle on my right, his name was Jerry Krisher, or a guy named Jim Schumacher who was the left tackle, "Come on Jim, get up to the line."

If I mentioned his name, that meant I was going to throw a quick pass to the tight end on his side.

Late in the game our defense stopped them just short of scoring. We took over on offense inside our own ten yard line. They bunched up the defense to keep us in the hole and lined up in that seven diamond.

Well, twice I hollered the tackles names and threw that look-in pass to our tight ends. Even though it was successful both times, my passing so deep in our own territory scared our coaches to death.

Although it got us out of the hole, the coaches realized they needed better parameters for their checkoff system. I can imagine now, if my quarterback did that, the kind of shock it would put me in. Chuck Mather has mentioned that many times, especially at banquets where he has introduced me.

The only touchdown of the game came on an audible of sorts. Coach Mather sent in a play, but I changed it in the huddle. I called for a play that the whole team, for some reason, seemed to sense was going to produce a winner for us. Ace Crable was the ball carrier and it resulted in a touchdown, and that was the ball game and the state championship.

There were some pictures on the front page of the paper the next day and Carol and I were both in them. She was in the band holding up a sign saying "Still State Champs". I was in a locker room picture as a 16-year-old quarterback with a beard. I had started growing the beard after our only loss and said I wouldn't shave until we were state champs. That was an exciting day for me and our team.

The game was played in the same stadium that is now used for the Hall of Fame game the pros play each year in Canton. It seats over 20,000, and it was sold out.

At our home field in Massillon we often played in front of 20,000 fans. One time we had 40,000 in Cleveland Stadium. We outdrew most of the small colleges in the state. The stadium is now named after Paul Brown, who later coached at Ohio State and for the Cincinnati Bengals. He coached my older brother Tommy in high school, at Ohio State University and with the Cleveland Browns. Tommy used to babysit Coach Brown's children when he was at Ohio State. And he was a pallbearer at Paul Brown's funeral.

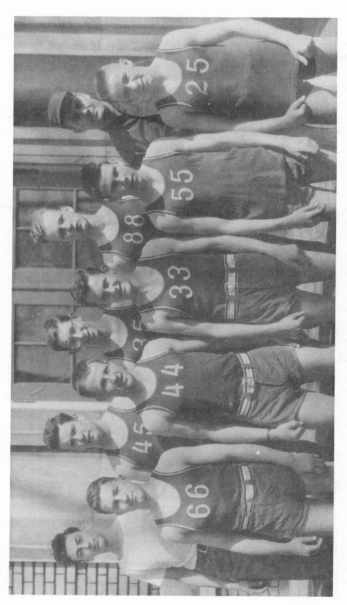

Our junior high basketball team.

Front row, from the left: Dick Shine, Dick Jacobs, Howard Welsh, Don Slicker, then me. Back row: Our student manager, Jerry Prisher, Chuck McMasters, Bob Henderhan and Coach Bill Muir.

I was in one of the best high school programs in America. It was very structured with a lot of emphasis on fitness and a good year around concept. My coaches were the kind of people I wanted to be like.

The Canton-Massillon area is still a hotbed for high school sports. Massillon was in the playoffs again this past year. But now they have a playoff system in Ohio and no longer name a mythical champion.

Despite quarterbacking our team to a state championship, I wasn't highly recruited. As I look back on it, I wouldn't recruit myself nowadays either. Who is going after a 5-foot-9-inch, 150 pound quarterback?

But there were 50-some colleges and universities in Ohio and 30 of them played football. So I was hoping to get a scholarship offer from somebody. Of course I thought I was better than the college coaches thought I was. I was only 16 years old my senior season in high school.

Football was my main sport. I played basketball early, but couldn't make varsity so I dropped that. I ran track as a sophomore because I couldn't make the baseball team. I wanted to be a baseball player, however, so I moved to that sport the spring of my junior and senior seasons.

I was an infielder. I never really thought I'd have any kind of a future as a pro, although I guess I was better than average. I batted left-handed and had good quickness, so I could beat out some ground balls. I think if I had devoted as much time to baseball as I did to football I could at least have gone on in that sport to the college level.

I was an above average student. I guess that showed by my ability to later get my master's degree in one year at Kansas. That was a pretty heavy study load while also coaching. My high school grades probably weren't all that great. But I knew they would be good enough to get into college so I didn't study as hard as I

could have or should have. The GPA wasn't as important then as it is now.

I took enough college preparatory courses in math,
sciences, and foreign language to qualify for college.
But the biggest influence on me came from my coaches
more than my teachers.

We had a great high school coaching staff. Massillon had six coaches for the high school team — Chuck
Mather, Dave Putts, Ducky Schroeder, Dick Piskoty,
Lauri Wartinian and Paul Schroeder. I decided then
and there that those were the people I wanted to be like
and that's what I wanted to do with my life. However,
when I went to college, I knew I not only wanted to be
a coach but I wanted to coach at the college level.

chapter eight

*A scholarship offer
allowed me to join Carol
at the University of Miami*

During our senior year in high school, as I said earlier, Carol's doctor had suggested she go to college where the weather was warm. She applied and was accepted at the University of Miami in Florida.

There had been a rumor in the fall that someone knew a scout who was going to try to get me a scholarship there, but even after the season was over, I hadn't heard from anyone. I had pretty much decided to go to Kiski Prep School in Pennsylvania.

Just before graduation in May, Bob Brietenstein made a late spring trip through Ohio. He had just been hired to the Miami staff by head coach Andy Gustafson.

Brietenstein, who became the running back coach at Miami, had been the head coach at Shaker High School in Shaker Heights, Ohio. After talking to me, Bob offered me a one-year scholarship to Miami. But he made it plain that there was no guarantee it would be renewed.

Brietenstein also offered a scholarship to a Massillon teammate named Walt Houston. Robin Brown, Paul Brown's son, was a third Ohio high school senior who also got a Miami scholarship. Robin played his high school ball for Brietenstein at Shaker Heights.

I got to know Robin and his father Paul when his dad coached my older brother at Massillon High, later at Ohio State and with the Cleveland Browns. I believe that Paul Brown has to be one of the greatest coaches ever in the sport of football.

A scholarship back in those days was a better deal than the NCAA will let us offer now. In addition to room and board, books and tuition, we also had transportation included.

In addition to that, we each got $15 a month in what they called "laundry money". That was for incidentals that we might need — everything from a tube of toothpaste to a movie ticket. I had that all through my college career.

So, the three of us — Houston, Brown and I — got on the train and went down to Miami in August of 1950. The next spring they thought I had played well enough that they extended me to a full four year scholarship.

Walt Houston wasn't real happy down there and transferred to Purdue where his brother Jack was on the team. He later played one year of pro ball with the Washington Redskins in the NFL. But Walt was doing so well in business that he quit football. He has been very successful. His brothers, Jim and Lindell, were both great players with the Cleveland Browns.

Robin Brown was a tough football player. But he got a head injury his first year at Miami and that was the end of his football career.

Later, Walt Houston and Robin Brown were both in our wedding party.

Andy Gustafson was the head coach at Miami all through my career there. Coach Gustafson was an old Pittsburgh fullback. He came to Miami from Colonel

Blaik's staff at Army. He was a very bright man and very articulate. I used to look forward to his pep talks. The problem was that his best talks came when we were on a losing streak.

Freshmen were not eligible at that time so we played a regular freshman schedule my first year. There was a lot of attrition in those days. They didn't have the scholarship limits that the NCAA imposes on us now. There were 45 recruited players in my freshman class. But only five of the 45 played as seniors four years later. We had a lot of guys that fell by the wayside.

A lot of schools "over-signed" in those days. Those were in the "runoff" days. Everybody would bring in 40-70 guys. Many of the marginal players would get discouraged and quit when they saw they weren't going to make it. Or the coaches would make it so difficult for them that they would in effect run them off.

In those days it seemed like you either stayed in school and graduated or you left college, never to return. There were not many players coming back later to finish once they quit school. Guys who fell by the wayside just didn't graduate. Of course the pressure on the GPA was not near what it is today. To get into some graduate programs — with the possible exception of medical school or law school — was not all that difficult.

Now, it takes a good GPA just to get into a college and a better one to get into a degree program after your first two years. In those days there was not that kind of academic competition.

Miami had a good team my freshman year. That was the year that Purdue broke Notre Dame's long winning streak. Then Miami beat Purdue and we went to the Orange Bowl that year.

I was the third team quarterback my sophomore year. Jackie Hackett was the starter. Bob Schneidenbach was second. We had some real good

Carol and I were married on August 9, 1952 following our
sophomore year at the University of Miami.

talent and earned a bid to the Gator Bowl against Clemson.

We had a break after the regular season ended and most of the students had gone home for Christmas. I was over at the locker room looking at the bulletin board. There was a new bowl trip roster on the board and my name wasn't on it. It had been earlier. The coaches had told me that I was going to go to the Gator Bowl game.

I think I learned something about compassion for players from that experience. That's no way to let a college sophomore know that he's not going on a bowl trip. We didn't have that many players and I was the third team quarterback. But, for budget reasons, they slashed the travel roster to a bare minimum. What was almost as bad as not making the bowl trip, was that I missed some of the Christmas break. I hadn't planned to go home since I was going to the bowl game.

I earned the job as the starting quarterback my final two seasons at Miami. In my first game as the starter we beat VMI, 45-0.

My first losing game was to Kentucky, where Bear Bryant was the coach. After that game The Bear told the press, "That Don James is a good passing quarterback." I still have that clipping in a scrapbook. That was quite a compliment.

In those last two seasons I managed to set five school passing records.

Three single season records came my junior year — most completions, 82; most passing yardage, 913; and passes attempted, 144.

I threw four touchdown passes that year and ran for two more. Obviously, since lots of guys nowadays will have four TD passes in a single game, the records I set as a Hurricane have long since been broken by the likes of Vinnie Testeverde, Jim Kelly, Steve Walsh and Bernie Kosar.

But I felt my junior year was good. My 53 percent completion average, a season high at Miami, ranked me eighth in the nation. The number of passes completed was 18th in the country.

My senior year I was 82 of 144 for 913 yards. Those were all new one season records at Miami. As was the percentage of completions. That year I was 5th in the nation on percentage of passes completed.

I also padded my career completions record to 121 in 219 attempts for 1,363 yards. That broke the previous records held by Jack Hackett.

In one game that season against Richmond, I completed 9 of 11 for 154 yards and one touchdown. Prior to that, only three passers in Miami history had more than 9 completions in a game. Of the two incompletions, the newspaper the next day said that "a Richmond back was able to deflect one and the Miami receiver dropped the other after having it in his hands."

It's kind of funny when you think about it now. Nine of 11. That was a big passing day back then.

I certainly didn't expect to follow my older brother Tommy into the NFL but I would have liked to. Tommy was a running back and a defensive star at Ohio State and joined the Cleveland Browns in 1948. That was when the Browns won six division titles. Tommy earned three championship rings and gained additional notoriety as the holder for kicking legend Lou Groza. Tommy finished his career as a pro player in 1955.

I did get a letter of inquiry from the Pittsburgh Steelers when I finished my senior season,. Following Tommy's footsteps into the NFL had been a longtime goal of mine, but I knew there weren't many 5-foot-9-inch quarterbacks in the NFL. Looking back on it, though, if I hadn't had that goal, I probably wouldn't have gone as far as I did.

I realize 5-9 was even short for a college quarterback, although the linemen weren't as big back then, so I could still see down field. However, to com-

pensate for my lack of height, the coaches devised a lot
of rollout plays.

When Dale Samuels was at Purdue and they beat
Notre Dame and we then beat Purdue, we had some
film on Purdue. That's when our coaches put in the rollout series because Dale wasn't very tall either. The
deep rolls would get me out on the corner where I could
spot the receivers better. I don't remember that we had
very many drop back passes, if any.

The NCAA had some strange rules my last two
years. You had to play both offense and defense and if
you came out, you couldn't go back in during that same
quarter. It was a few years later that Coach Paul Dietzel at LSU had his 'White' team, the 'Go' team and his
'Chinese Bandits'. His 'White' team played both ways
— offense and defense. The 'Go' team specialized in offense, while the defensive specialist, who usually went
in to finish up each quarter, were called the 'Chinese
Bandits'.

Because of those rules, if I started when we first
got the ball and that initial drive stalled, I either had to
play defense or come out. If I came out, we would substitute a good defensive back and the second team
quarterback would go in the next time we got the ball.
I couldn't go in again until the second quarter.

But it was a fun experience. We played all of our
home games in the Orange Bowl, just as they still do.

Not too many games from my college career stick
out in my mind. One that does, however, was the time
we went up to New York to play Fordham in the Polo
Grounds. Another was when we went to Boston and
played Boston College when they had Harry Agganis,
the Golden Greek. That game was in Fenway Park. It
was a real highlight to play in those two great old
stadiums.

One other game is particularly vivid. My junior
year we played Georgia. They had a young quarterback
named Zeke Bratkowski who eventually broke Babe

We graduated from Miami together in the
spring of 1954

Parilli's NCAA passing record. They beat us 35-13 and Zeke and I had the ball in the air all night. I think I threw as many times as he did. I can't remember the numbers, but it was also one of my better days.

The Florida game was a big rival game each year. I wish I could say that I threw a 'Hail Mary' pass in the final six seconds to win those games. The truth of the matter is that we didn't win many games during my junior and senior seasons.

There weren't too many guys from my class that I kept in close contact with after college because we moved so much. Dan Tassotti, a big tackle from the Pittsburgh area, was one. He later moved out to Seattle, but died of a heart attack a couple of years ago. We sure miss Big Dan and his wife, Inez.

I suppose some of that lack of closeness was because, as a married student, I didn't hang around with many of my teammates. Also, after finishing school, I became so far removed from the area while many of the others continued to live in Florida.

When we went back to play Oklahoma in the Orange Bowl in 1985 we used the University of Miami facilities for our practices. I got to see some of my college teammates as they dropped by to watch us workout.

chapter nine

The Army to Kansas,
a high school job,
and then Florida State

I was in college during the Korean Conflict. Because of the standard two-year military commitment, I added ROTC to my schedule. It was a real incentive to stay in school and get your commission.

Although the "conflict" — it sounded like a war to me — was over by the time I graduated. But, because of ROTC, I had the two-year service commitment to fulfill.

Upon graduation I was sent to Fort Eustis, Virginia, where I went through the transportation school. I also played football for the post team that next fall.

It was a great team. We had Johnny Coatta, the former Wisconsin quarterback, and T. Jones from Texas. We also had guys from Tennessee and several other major schools. Some of them went on to pro ball.

That was probably my best year of football. I could see my age and experience catching up with me. My arm was stronger. During that fall we didn't have too many duties other than playing for the team.

Our outfit won the camp intermural trophy after I was
assigned to Camp LeRoy Johnson in New Orleans.

As soon as the season was over we jumped right back into the transportation school. When I finished, I was assigned to the Army Port of Embarkation in New Orleans. It was out on Lake Ponchetrain. They had a small camp named Camp LeRoy Johnson. It's since been torn down.

I also kept an association with sports while I was there. I was the baseball coach for the camp team. We enjoyed our time there. Carol and I met a lot of interesting people, many of whom we still keep in contact with.

There was the Mardi Gras. And we would go into the French Quarter a lot. At least we did until we acquired our first parental responsibilities. Our son Jeff was born in 1955 while we were in New Orleans.

I was discharged from the service in the spring of 1956. Even before that I had been keeping in touch with Chuck Mather, my high school coach at Massillon. He had become the head coach at the University of Kansas.

I went right from the camp in New Orleans to summer school at Kansas to get started on my master's degree. Mather offered me job as a grad assistant with the Jayhawks.

I managed to get my master's degree in one complete school year. So I was at Kansas for just about one calendar year.

That was some schedule. Daughter Jill was born soon after we arrived. She is just 16 months younger than Jeff. So there we were, living in a house trailer with two small children. Except for the grad assistants pay, our only other income was from the GI Bill. Yet we thought we were rich.

My title was offensive backfield coach for the freshman team. Wayne Replogle was the head freshman coach, but he did a lot of the scouting for the varsity. A good bit of the time I was actually in charge of the freshman team. Norm Stoppel was also a grad assistant. He's out of coaching, but he's still in Kansas in business.

It was fun for me to be a part of the Big Eight Conference — although at that time the media referred to it as Oklahoma and the Seven Dwarfs when it came to football.

But Kansas had a lot of great athletes. Al Orter, the many-time Olympic Gold medalist discus thrower, was on the track team, while Wilt Chamberlain was a freshman on the basketball team.

Chuck was just getting the football team going. It was his third year as the head coach. I think he lost every game his first year. But Kansas was starting to get more competitive.

I enjoyed my first coaching experience. After all, here was a former quarterback coaching the offensive backs. My biggest contributions as an assistant coach probably came at Florida State, Michigan and Colorado as a defensive coordinator.

After I earned my master's degree, I only got involved in one coaching job opening at the college level. That was an assistant's job at New Mexico. When I didn't get that I had a chance to become a coach on the staff at Southwest High School back in Miami. I was there for two seasons.

At the high school level I taught physical education and a general math class. When I was hired, the principal asked me if I could teach math. I told him I didn't have any experience at it, but as it turned out, I enjoyed it.

It was a new school, but we had pretty good teams the two years I was there. We had winning records both seasons.

Bob Breitenstein, who recruited me out of high school to go to Miami, was still living there. Carol and I saw him quite regularly. After my second year at the high school, Perry Moss was hired at Florida State.

Breitenstein knew Moss and told me he had suggested to Perry that he should interview me.

I was invited to go up to Tallahassee for an interview the next Saturday. While I was gone, Carol went to Hollywood, Florida, to stay with her folks at their winter home. They had just arrived and didn't have a telephone yet. When I got hired I couldn't even share the good news with her.

She told me that on Sunday morning she went out to get the newspaper off the front porch and read that I'd been hired. That's how she found out I'd gotten my first fulltime college coaching job.

We moved to Tallahassee on February 14th. Carol has always said that was the best Valentine present she ever received.

Moss was only at Florida State one year before leaving to take over the Montreal Alouettes of the Canadian Football League. Then Bill Peterson came to Florida State from LSU and I spent six more seasons with him.

chapter ten

*Developing a coaching
philosophy and the
Bryant-Butts story*

Bill Peterson was an offensive-minded coach. He
wanted to open things up and throw it. We went into a
lot of games as the underdog in those years.

It's fairly normal, if you are consistently an underdog, to use either a lot of option plays or pass a lot. You
do that to try and make up for the physical strength advantage of your opponent.

Because offense was his main interest, when Bill
became the head coach at Florida State I ended up over
on defense. Ken Meyer was the defensive coordinator.
He is a former head coach of the San Francisco 49ers
and is now the quarterback coach of the Seattle
Seahawks.

Ken went from Florida State to Alabama and spent
a few years with Bear Bryant. He's an outstanding
coach. The Southeast Conference, at that time, was a
great arena in which to learn. I got a taste of Bobby
Dodd and General Nyland's philosophy on defense and
the kicking game. Then there was Coach Bryant's phi-

losophy of hard-nosed aggressive play combined with great speed and quickness.

I think we all adapted our off-season program philosophy to the quickness and intensity of the game as The Bear coached it. The idea was to get each young man to give you a four to six-second sellout in all of our drill work. That would translate to doing the same on game day.

Then there was the fundamental idea of playing great defense and the kicking game philosophy which came from Nyland and Dodd. I agreed with the need to have a sound kicking game but didn't want to be punting on third down, which they sometimes did. And I did not agree with the use of the quick kick. I've seen too many of them either get blocked or kicked poorly. The biggest impact on the coaching philosophy of defense that I developed came more from the Coach Bryant approach.

Then there was Paul Dietzel, who had worked for Colonel Blaik, Sid Gillman and Bear Bryant. After that he went to LSU and won a national championship in 1958. Bill Peterson was on that staff as the offensive line coach.

When Bill came to Florida State in 1960, he brought a lot of the Paul Dietzel philosophy of program development with him. It was very sound. It was highly detailed and organized. It included a year-around concept of developing a program.

We had a plan for everything. We kept our players together. We bed checked them the year around. We had a training table. It was one of the first programs to fully utilize academic counselors. We had a man outside the coaching staff in charge of seeing that the players all got in the right classes. And we had tutors and a study table.

We also hired a recruiting coordinator and worked to make the best possible use of the grad assistants. I think that's an important part of my present coaching

The Florida State coaching staff in 1964.

From the left: Bobby Bowden, now the FSU head coach, me, head coach Bill Peterson, Bill Crutchfield and John Coatta.
Back row: Don Powell, Bob Harbison, Bill Proctor, Y.C. McNease.

style which I got from Bill Peterson. The way to lay out a good solid program, how to organize it, and how to administer it.

Basically, we used the calendar year and plugged in what we thought a college football player should be doing every week of the year. Whether it was running, lifting weights, or working on position skills. I was at Florida State for seven years, the last six with Peterson and I could see how this strong organization was improving our team.

And I still use the same basic approach. It has changed some. Now we work it into an academic calendar on the quarter system. It starts each year about two weeks before fall camp opens with our staff meetings all outlined.

Then comes the in-season philosophy where you go through a typical week preparing the team. Then a bowl philosophy, a weight lifting philosophy while you're recruiting, following by a detailed plan on how the winter program will be conducted.

Then we come back with the spring practice plan. For the summer we have designed a fitness program. It starts while the players are still on campus. They maintain that program while at home for the summer and if they follow it religiously they will return in the fall in great shape and ready to begin fall camp.

During the summer they mail back the workout cards we give them so we have a record on their progress.

Now, we are into strength training and nutrition a good bit more than the kind of plan we followed in 1960. I don't think we're doing a whole lot better job than we did back then on the development of quickness. But we've added a speed class. I think we're doing a better job there. It gives you another way to build cardiovascular conditioning and endurance.

I digress a little, but when I think of that period of my career when I was first involved in Southeast foot-

ball I'm reminded of our involvement in the famous —
or infamous — Bear Bryant-Wally Butts trial.

I don't know if you remember the incident or not,
but there was an insurance man who picked up his
phone to make a call only to overhear a conversation
going on between Butts and Bryant. It was some kind
of a mixup in the phone company lines.

It was the year after Butts had left Georgia. The
accusation was that Butts was giving Coach Bryant a lot
of information about Georgia football to help Alabama
win the game. As I recall, the claim was that Butts and
Bryant were trying to fix a college game. Before all the
smoke cleared, there was the accusation of collusion in
throwing college football games.

In those years, Florida State also played Georgia.
We wound up in the investigation because we also beat
them after Y.C. McNeese, who was our middle guard,
intercepted a shovel pass on a play they were running
for the very first time.

There apparently had been a phone call logged
from Butts to someone at Florida State. The claim was
that Y.C. knew the play was coming. Obviously, I
would contend that McNeese was just a well-coached
middle guard.

The accusation was that Butts would watch Georgia
practices throughout the week before a game, learn
what the Bulldogs' game plan was going to be and then
call the opposing coach.

But, after all the investigation, they never did prove
that Butts "fixed" any games and he did receive a large
settlement from the Saturday Evening Post magazine
which broke the story.

McNeese became a part of the coaching staff at
Michigan while I was there. He later became the head
coach at the University of Idaho.

But back to my start as a defensive coach under Peterson at Florida State. My first couple of years I was
the assistant in charge of the defensive backs. Then I

Our defensive front at Florida State, known as the 'Seven Magnificents' with their shaved heads, pose in front of the defensive backs who were nicknamed 'The Fourgotten Four'.

In the back row, from the left: Maury Bibent, Jim Massey, Winfred Bailey and Howard Ehler. The 'Magnificents' from the left are George D'Allessandro, Frank Pennie, Dick Hermann, Jack Shinholser, Bill McDowell, Avery Sumner and Max Wettstein.

moved into the defensive coordinator's role. I continued to coach the defense backs after I became the coordinator.

We had a great group. In four seasons as the defensive coordinator, we posted 13 shutouts, held three other teams to just a field goal and 14 others to just one touchdown.

In 1964, my next-to-last year as Florida State's defensive coordinator, we were first in the national statistics in fumble recoveries, third in defense against the rush, fifth in overall defense, seventh in defense versus scoring and ninth in punt coverage.

That year our defense allowed just 75 yards a game rushing, caused 32 fumbles and recovered 23. Obviously, I think defense is very important. Our Rose Bowl team this past season was first in eight defensive categories in the Pac-10.

That particular Florida State defense featured a lot of tough kids. The linemen and linebackers showed up one day with shaved heads. They called themselves the Seven Magnificants. They were George D'Allesandre, Frank Pennie, Dick Hermann, Bill McDowell, Avery Sumner, Max Wettstein and Jack Shinholser.

Shinholser, our all-American middle guard, was one of the best.

Jack was great. In fact, he was so good that the Houston Veer was perfected and became a potent option offense because of him.

When we went over to play the Houston Cougars, we were running an angle defense. What Houston Coach Bill Yeoman decided to do with his dive back — since they could pretty much predict which way we were going to angle because of the tight end — they would double down on Jack and then bring their tackle down on our linebacker. If our tackle looped to the outside, which he normally did, they wouldn't block him, and they'd run that fullback dive in there and it was wide open.

But, if our tackle came inside, they'd pull the ball out from the dive back and go wide. I really think that the triple option philosophy of the Houston Veer came about because of Jack Shinholser.

We had not seen that blocking pattern before we played Houston and Bill Yeoman later told me that they designed this plan to take care of our fine middle guard.

The officials had not seen the play either. On one occasion, when the wing official started in to spot the ball after the fullback was tackled, he — the official — knocked our cornerback down. The ref didn't know it, but they had pulled the ball out on that play and ran wide. With our cornerback knocked down, they scored their only touchdown. And the game ended in a tie.

That's the kind of thing that comes back to haunt you. When it comes to coaching defensive backs, there isn't as much change in that phase of the game as you might think from 1960 to now. Especially in one-on-one man coverage. The things we were teaching then, people are still using.

We were in a lot of three deep zones then. Perry Moss was a master of secondary coaching in zone coverage. I sat in on the defensive meetings with Perry. He seemed just like an artist when he got to talking with a piece of chalk and a blackboard.

It was that experience that put me in a good position to move over to the defense when Peterson came in. What Moss was teaching we are still using. He was a good football coach.

I always thought high school football in eastern Ohio around Massillon or western Pennsylvania around the coal mine territory was tough. But each team seemed to have only two or three really tough guys. You go down to South Georgia to a high school game and you'll see a whole team of great hitters. They love the contact. That's the way these kids were. They'd really stick you.

Toward the end of my career at Florida State we would take a spring trip to visit other college programs. One spring we went over to LSU, where Peterson had been. Bill Beals was their defensive coordinator. I told him we were going to be playing Baylor the next fall. They had played Baylor the previous season and I asked Beals for a tip that might help.

He gave me what I thought was a revolutionary defense. It was a two deep, five underneath zone scheme. We went back and introduced it to our team. Then saved it for the Baylor game. And we won.

A year later, I became the defensive coordinator at Michigan and installed the same defense for a game against Purdue when Bob Griese was their quarterback. Griese took Purdue to the Rose Bowl that year, but we held him to just 63 yards passing on the day we played him.

Needless to say, I was really excited to be holding a great passer like Bob Griese to such a low yardage total at halftime. I told the defense they had played a great first half, but warned them that in the second half Griese would really fill the ball with air. Just a slight mixup of the tongue.

A lot of people live in that coverage now. It's a scheme with two deep zone defenders and four or five underneath short zone players. Most teams will also change up with the five short defenders picking up the receivers man-to-man with two deep safeties playing zones over the top.

Michigan had the best secondary I ever coached. Rick Volk, who was 6-3 and weighed 192, went on to a great career with the Baltimore Colts. Mike Bass was an equally valuable defensive back for years with the Washington Redskins. John Rowser, who was one of the best hitters I ever coached, played with the Pittsburgh Steelers. The fourth was Rick Sygar. Rick was a really bright student and a very fine college football player. He was the only one who didn't go into pro ball.

But there's one thing about pass defense. I don't care what kind of coverage you devise, if the opposing quarterback is pretty good and if you give him too much time, he'll pick you apart. You've got to have some rush.

We threw the ball a lot at Florida State, particularly when we had Steve Tensi passing to Fred Biletnikoff. Others were doing the same thing. Joe Namath was at Alabama. And Steve Spurrior was at Florida. We had to defend the whole field against all the formations that you see today. We had to be in a number of different coverages and had to play well if you wanted to be successful.

Nowadays, the NFL is a good resource for us, especially with so many games on TV. If anybody develops a new, good offensive concept, you'll find the defensive people quickly coming up with a counter move.

The new thing today is running the ball from the one-back offense. People are spreading the defense even more while at the same time retaining the ability to run the ball. That's the biggest change in the past few years. Philosophically, defensive coaches said nobody is going to beat me running the ball with only one back. But the Redskins proved that it can happen. We'd been in one-back offense for years and years, but our one-back running offense was restricted to a draw play. With the new changes, however, we can now attack about every hole with one back.

chapter eleven

*I was the defensive coordinator
at both Michigan and Colorado
before my first head coaching job*

We played excellent defense while I was the coordinator at Florida State. But seven years at Florida State was probably long enough.

I wasn't really looking for a move, but an opportunity arose that certainly demanded consideration.

Bump Elliott had just taken Michigan to the Rose Bowl. But after that game he lost Bob Holloway, his defensive coordinator, and Don Dufek, his secondary coach, to other jobs.

Tony Mason, who was a good friend of mine, was on that staff. Tony was a very successful high school coach in Ohio and a very gifted speaker. Bump had hired him as a line coach. He later became the head coach at Cincinnati and Arizona. I didn't know Bump, but Tony suggested that he look at me as a possible candidate. Then Bump called.

I'll never forget going up there for my interview. Michigan is such a great university and football school.

It's some feeling to go into that stadium. There's no college stadium like it in the country. It's very impressive.

Carol was also impressed. They flew both of us up there, which was somewhat unusual for an assistant's job.

When I was ready to leave for the Michigan interview, I got a call from Georgia Tech. I called Bobby Dodd from the Atlanta airport to tell him I was on my way to Michigan.

Fritz Crisler was still the athletic director at Michigan. Of course, that was real impressive. The Fritz Crisler mystique. He had also been a great coach at Michigan.

If there was a negative about him, it was that after he became the athletic director he didn't keep pace with what others were doing in football. Instead, he kept things pretty much as they had been when he coached.

At one time he had been the athletic director, football coach and head of the physical education department. As a result, we didn't have as big a football staff as many of our competitors.

When I got to Michigan they had fewer coaches than probably any school in the Big Ten, maybe any major Division I school in the country. They had fewer projectors for film study and no graduate assistants. One of our assistants was part-time football and part-time wrestling. We had like five guys coaching. Everybody else had so many more they were beating us in recruiting as well as coaching.

Despite those disadvantages, Michigan had a consistently winning program. Because of that success it was hard to sell Crisler on the idea that we needed more people, projectors and other things. Fritz even had a mileage limitation on our recruiting trips. As a result, Duffy Daugherty at Michigan State was getting good players from Texas that we couldn't even recruit.

And so it was that I was hired to replace both the defensive secondary coach and the defensive coordinator.

Fritz was an extremely articulate and bright man, however. When he got in front of the department to talk or when he spoke at a banquet, he was spellbinding.

We made the move from Florida State in February, soon after we had beaten Oklahoma in the Gator Bowl. Carol and our two young children joined me right away. Whenever I made a change, we both felt it was important that she pick up and join me as soon as possible. She felt that whenever I moved to a new job, there were enough pressures with the job that we needed to have the family together. It was sometimes hard on our children because new coaching jobs usually come open at the end of the football season, which means the middle of the school year. But we always felt it was important to keep the family together.

When I first got to Michigan, Benny Oosterbaun gave me a copy of Fielding Yost's book to read. It was written in 1905. Here was another legend who had coached the Wolverines. The book didn't tell how to defend the pass. But it's amazing. The basic fundamentals of life haven't changed much over the years. And the same can be said about football. Neither has the technique on how to block and tackle.

In addition to being a great coach, Yost was an engineer. He designed Michigan's 101,000-seat stadium. He fixed it so the water from the stadium area drains over across the road to form a lake on the university golf course. Then they water the course from the lake.

The fun part of being at Michigan was the opportunity to work with Bump Elliott and Fritz Crisler.

Bump was a real positive leader, a polite, pleasant person. He had to be one of the world's great human beings.

But my stay at Michigan was short. Just two seasons. You'd think there would never be a reason for a person to want to leave Michigan. But a rather delicate situation arose.

Fritz Crisler announced that he was going to retire. Immediately, rumors began to float around. Was Bump going to keep his football job or would he become the athletic director? Or, would somebody else come in and clean house?

Don Canham was the track coach and a very successful business man. There was a rumor that he'd be the athletic director and he'd bring in all his own people.

As each day went by it became more and more apparent that Bump was not going to be the athletic director. Also, that Bo Schemblechler was being heavily considered to be the coach and Don Canham would be the AD. That certainly meant that the jobs of all the assistants were going to be in jeopardy.

About that time I got a call from Woody Hayes. He had an opening at Ohio State. I went down and spent four hours in an interview with him. After the long visit, however, I just didn't think my temperament would be all that compatible with Woody Hayes. There were a lot of stories about how volatile he was, especially with his coaches.

In the meantime, Eddie Crowder at Colorado, who had a good year the season before and had gone to a bowl game, lost his secondary coach, Billy Williamson and Rudy Feldman, his defensive coordinator. Feldman had become the head coach at New Mexico.

It was the same situation that had arisen at Michigan. Two assistants leaving with a defensive secondary position open as well as the title of defensive coordinator.

While getting suggestions on people he might consider, Crowder had talked to Woody. And Coach Hayes had mentioned me. Quite a bit of time passed before anything materialized. Although Eddie first talked to me in January, I didn't go out to Boulder until March,

I still didn't want to leave Michigan, but because of the situation there, when I was offered the job as defensive coordinator at Colorado, I finally agreed to take it.

Although it may have seemed to many to be just a lateral move and not a real career advancement, it was for a good bit more money. In fact, Carol and I thought we could live comfortably the rest of our lives on that initial salary.

The year after I went to Colorado, Bump had a great 8-2 season, yet he was released. Bump then went to Iowa as the athletic director and helped build one of the most competitive athletic programs in the country. With those changes, I have no idea where I might have fit into the picture at either Michigan or Iowa — if at all. I'm sure it was a good thing I left as I would have no doubt been out of a job. And, best of all, we loved Colorado.

We had three good years at Colorado before my first head coaching opportunity came up and I went to Kent State.

Two of those seasons we played in the Liberty Bowl. In the first of those games we played Bear Bryant and beat him.

I'll never forget a situation that came up in the Liberty Bowl game that involved The Bear. In that game, Alabama ran the Utah shovel pass against us. The halfback dropped the ball and one of our players fell on it. The ref ruled it a fumble and gave us the ball.

Coach Bryant ran on the field to complain. He was right, of course. It should have been ruled an incomplete pass. Well, he talked the refs into changing their ruling. It was an incomplete pass and Alabama maintained possession. Then the ref walked off 15 yards against The Bear for coming on the field.

That put Alabama deep in its own end of the field and on the next play we sacked the quarterback for a safety. And those two points made the difference in the final score and won the game for Colorado.

I can still see The Bear out there, getting the ruling changed and then getting slapped with a 15-yard penalty even though he was right. That was really bizarre. After the safety, of course, they had a free kick. And they had their punter in there. But we didn't have our punt receivers in. We had our kickoff receiving team on the field. We had never given it any thought. In my whole coaching career I don't think anybody had ever covered that. And the kick-off receiver fumbled the punt. But, fortunately, we recovered it and hung on to the lead for the victory.

It's experiences like that which help you learn. After 20 years I continue to learn. I had never thought about not having the kickoff team in after a safety. Yet fielding a kickoff and fielding a punt requires a totally different skill. It's catching a different kind of ball. It's a minor detail, but it's something that has stuck with me.

At Colorado, we had been into multiple defenses. Some years we've tried to simplify it, adjusting the defense to our personnel. The Oklahoma fifty defense or 5-2-4 has been around so long. Clear back to the Bud Wilkinson days. A lot of coaches still use it as a base. Many similarities still exist.

This past year we were more of a blitz team at Washington. But the basic techniques of defense are much the same as when I was first the coordinator at Florida State. Basically what a blitz does is put your secondary in man-to-man coverage. Now the question is, can your defensive backs cover long enough until the front people get some pressure on the quarterback? The thing that has happened with the passing game is that we have always had checkoffs. But now, if you see the strong safety starting to rotate up for a strong safety crash, coaches are doing a better job with a scheme against the blitz. We devote 10 minutes at every practice working our quarterbacks, with a clock, on what to do against a blitz or crash. We refer to linebacker pressure as a blitz and pressure from the defensive backfield as a crash.

I made our coaches put a clock on our quarterbacks in practice last year because they were having trouble with the 25-second time limit. Now we practice with a clock every day so they will have a better feel for it during a game.

The other big thing that has happened to offensive football is our sight adjustment plays. If some defensive safety comes up to blitz so late that my quarterback can't check it off and audible to a new play, but he can see the blitz coming and so can our receiver, then the receiver will run a pre-determined route based on what he sees.

I'm sure such a tactic is even more sophisticated in the NFL. They — the quarterbacks and the receivers — are so skilled. And also, they don't have academics to worry about. They basically have the whole day to devote to refining their skills. They can do a lot more. Although it's interesting, when you look at the Super Bowl, the successful teams seem to be the ones that do the least. Keep it simple, but do what they do very well.

The Washington Redskins have proven that theory. They run just three or four plays. But they run them well. They make you stop them. They seldom stop themselves.

That bowl game at Colorado against The Bear led us to several other subjects. Getting back to my time in Boulder, having come from the Southeast and then the Big Ten, there was no question in my mind that in those years the Big Eight was the strongest conference in the country. The speed and size of the players in the league was incredible. I was really impressed.

One game that really stands out was our home game against Penn State. They had beaten us back there the year before. We had a pretty good team coming back and they did too. But we had them at our place on national TV. And that's when we broke their 30-some game winning streak, which was the longest in the country. After doing that, we were on the cover of Sports Illustrated the next week.

I remember walking into a restaurant with Eddie Crowder after the game and getting a standing ovation. Football was king in that conference at that time.

The next year, after I had left for Kent State, the Big Eight went 1-2-3 in the final polls. Nebraska was 13-0 and national champion. Oklahoma's only loss was to Nebraska. And Colorado's only losses were to Nebraska and Oklahoma. And all three teams were victorious in the Orange, Sugar and Cotton Bowls.

One other game that stands out in my memory was a Colorado game against the Air Force. They had earned the right to play in the Cotton Bowl the previous week. And they had just beaten Stanford, a team that was to be the Pac-8 representative in the Rose Bowl at the end of that season. We went down to the Academy in Colorado Springs for the game.

I thought we had an outstanding game plan. Anyway, we got the ball and marched all the way down to inside their five. But, on an option, one of their defensive backs intercepted the pitchout and went 90-some yards for a touchdown.

They kicked off again and we march it again. We hammer it all the way down and score. The first quarter comes to an end. The score is tied 7-7 and our defense had yet to play a down.

The night before that game we took the team to see the movie "Patton". While we were at the movie, the Air Force cadets stole Ralphie, the Colorado buffalo mascot.

The next afternoon, our students came on the field with a chicken with a string tied around its neck — imitating their hawk. After that, they returned our Buffalo. We won that particular game and the series had quickly developed into an intense rivalry.

Boulder was a beautiful place. We liked the mountains. We skied. I think both Carol and I felt we would be happy to spend the rest of our lives there. While we were in Colorado, Jeff and Jill were in junior high and Jeni was born in Boulder.

But an opportunity came along and after the Liberty Bowl game in 1970 it was announced that I'd been hired as the head coach at Kent State.

Most everyone told me, "Don't go. It's the graveyard of coaches." But you don't get that many chances to become a head coach and I felt that Kent State could become a good football school and that I could put together a staff that could win.

Another factor in favor of taking the job was the fact that Carol and I would be going back close to home for the first time since we left for college in 1950. We would be able to see our families a lot more than before. And that was important because both sets of parents were getting up in years. And it gave our children the chance to really get to know their grandparents.

chapter twelve

*Kent State: My first
head coaching job
was a 'Homecoming'*

For the first time in my career, after being named
the head coach at Kent State, I faced the task of hiring
my own staff.

I had received a lot of pointers on how to go about
that during my years as an assistant coach. Most people
believe that for your first staff as a head coach, you
should go with 90 percent new people. So I picked out
one holdover coach and was going to hire new assistants
to fill out the rest of the staff. As it turned out, the one
I planned to retain soon signed on as an assistant with a
Big Ten school, so I ended up with all new coaches.

I hired Denny Fitzgerald, who I knew from Michigan. He was then the defensive coordinator at Kentucky. I got him as my defensive coordinator. That
might not have even been a lateral move for him. It
might have been a down move. But Denny felt it was a
good opportunity in the long run for his career and I
was pleased to get him. I think maybe he wasn't too
sold on how things were going at Kentucky at the time.

He eventually became the head coach at Kent State and later moved to the NFL with the Pittsburgh Steelers. I think Dennis is out of coaching now.

I brought in Maury Bibent as my secondary coach. I had coached him at Florida State. He was from Cincinnati, Ohio, and had been a grad assistant at Michigan. I also hired Bob Stull, who is now the head coach at Missouri. Then there was Skip Hall, who was a grad assistant with us at Colorado. He is now the head coach at Boise State. And Ray Dorr, from Akron, Ohio, who is now the quarterback coach at USC. He was the head coach at Illinois State before that.

I hired Dick Scesniak from Utah as my offensive coordinator. He later came to Seattle with me, then went with the New York Giants, then Wisconsin, then back to Kent State as the head coach. He was there when he had a heart attack and died.

Another of my original Kent State assistants was Sam Elliott, who had been a grad assistant at Ohio State. He had walked on as a freshman at Ohio State, yet later became the captain of the team his senior year. And Fred Gissendaner from Akron, who had been a high school coach. I later added Greg Long, who was also from the Ohio area. I really had a great staff of young, aggressive, hard-working guys.

We became known as the "James Gang." The media picked up on that. As a result, for our press guides and other publicity, a lot of western themes were built around that. You know, "The James Gang rides again." "They don't rebuild, they reload." Things like that.

I arrived on the Kent State campus just seven months after the unfortunate confrontation between the students and the Ohio National Guard that led to "The Shooting".

When I got there and talked to the members of the coaching staff, they said there were not many real "players", but that I was inheriting a couple of very good ones that I could build the team around.

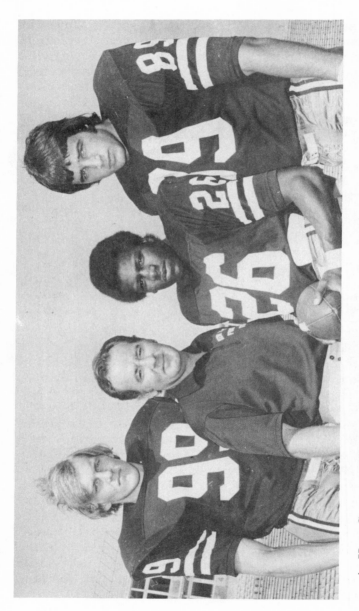

At Kent State in 1973 with (from left) Jack Lambert, who became an all- pro linebacker, Eddie Woodard and Gary Pinkel, who later was an assistant for me at Kent State and UW before becoming the head coach at the University of Toledo.

Both Gary Pinkel and Jack Lambert were on the freshman team together. Gary was an outstanding tight end. After he graduated he had a chance to play with the Steelers but gave it up in order to pursue a career in coaching. Now Gary is the head coach at Toledo.

Lambert was the most competitive player I have ever coached.

Jack was a defensive back-quarterback out of a small Ohio town. He wasn't recruited very heavily. In fact, he came to Kent State on a partial grant. He wasn't there very long, however, before he was on a full scholarship. You could see he was a player.

Lambert got thrown out of the first spring scrimmage we had after I got there. We brought in officials and they ejected him for fighting. I told the ref, "You don't throw guys out of a spring scrimmage. I'll handle that." Jack was a fierce competitor. He was so intense all the time. He just didn't want anybody to catch a pass in his zone or make any yardage in his direction, even if we were working in sweats. And best of all, it was contagious. He inspired the team. He'd get on his own teammates if he didn't think they were giving their best.

Not to put down Kent State, but some people still wonder why Lambert wasn't at Ohio State. The reason was his size. He wasn't very big. He only weighed 204 pounds as an NFL linebacker in his first Super Bowl. After his college career, even though he was drafted in the second round, there were skeptics who thought he was too light to play in the NFL.

I had one scout come by before the draft to watch us play. He told a reporter that Jack would never make it in the NFL because of his size. That infuriated me. I called the general manager of the team to complain. I told him I didn't care what the guy thinks, but he shouldn't be making public quotes about our players or any players.

This was back in the days when the NFL had the early draft, so the rest of the year before he graduated, Lambert drove over to Pittsburgh once a week to study film and get himself ready.

Jack may have been in that marginal category because of his size, but he fooled 'em. He became a starter as a rookie.

My first game as a head coach is still very memorable. We opened on the road against North Carolina State and won! They probably had us signed up as a warmup game. But we had every psychological advantage in the world.

First of all, we were a new staff and all pumped up. Secondly, when you face a new coach, you don't know what he's going to do. I'm sure the NC State staff had looked at a lot of Colorado film, feeling that I would install a system similar to the one I had most recently been involved with.

But I had told Dick Scesniak, when I gave him the offensive coordinator's job, "This is how we're going to start — we're going to run the 'I', the pro set and the two tight end formations. I want to run the basic 'I' plays and I want you to put it together. And get a passing attack."

I wanted to throw a little more than we had at Colorado to achieve a little better run-pass balance. Colorado was a real power running team. I felt we would be underdogs for a few years, so we needed to open up more with the passing game.

For that first game I think we did a fairly good job of coaching and our players went down there and played very well. They were particularly solid from the standpoint of no turnovers. They probably played over their heads. And we beat 'em, 23-21.

We arrived back home at the Akron airport around midnight after the game. A group of family, friends, neighbors and fans were there with banners to meet us.

For Kent State it was probably a first to welcome home the heroes.

But we were just 3-8 that first year. We started playing poor defense after that first game. We were giving up a lot of points. To be honest, we weren't very good. We had a pro style defense like the one we had at Colorado. Midway through the season I told the staff we needed to move the best defensive player we had to inside linebacker. That, of course, was Jack Lambert. He had been used at defensive end prior to my arrival.

If nothing else that first year, we found Jack's best position. He, of course, became one of the NFL's best-ever at linebacker and was recently inducted into the pro football Hall of Fame in Canton, Ohio. Lambert was our co-captain his senior year.

Our second season at Kent State we played Iowa State University and San Diego State. Our overall record wasn't all that great, but we did win the school's first — and only — conference championship.

Kent State had never won a Mid-American title before. After the season we took the team to Tampa and played in the Citrus Bowl. Back then it was called the Tangerine Bowl. We played the University of Tampa coached by Earle Bruce.

We were 9-2 my third year there, although we didn't win the title.

Kent State had an enrollment of over 20,000 students. It is Division 1-A, just like the schools in the Pac-10. The perception, however, is that the Mid-American Conference isn't really "big time". That comes from the fact that it labors under the umbrella of the Big Ten and Notre Dame.

It is a similar situation to Fresno State, San Jose State, Long Beach State, even San Diego State on the west coast. Most people back east probably think they are little schools who couldn't compete on the level of the schools in the Pac-10. Yet they are bigger and as good or better than some of the so-called "name" schools. They just don't enjoy the same national image because of their lack of visibility.

We put a lot of guys in the NFL from Kent State. Of course Lambert was the premier player, but there were a bunch of others, including running back Larry Poole, who played with the Browns and Cedric Brown, who was with Tampa for years. Also Larry Faulk with the Jets and Gerald Tinker, who won a gold medal in the Olympics. He could flat out fly.

When we recruited, we went after the best. If we lost one to a Big Ten school we'd tell 'em, "If things don't go well, remember us." After a year or two, several of them would transfer back to Kent State.

It was at Kent State that a long-lasting relationship with Mike Lude began. He had coached for Davey Nelson at Deleware, then became the head coach at Colorado State.

The first time I met Mike was the day of a Penn State game at Colorado. I had seen him the previous two years on his Sunday TV show, but he had lost his job at Colorado State. He was working with the Broncos and selling real estate in Denver, Colorado.

Mike was a good friend of Eddie Crowder. Since the Penn State game was a sellout, Eddie had given Mike a sideline pass. He was standing by the tunnel long before the kickoff when we came on the field for the first time. I just stopped to say hello and we had time to visit for quite a while.

Soon after that Mike was named the athletic director at Kent State. When he began looking for a new head coach I called and asked if I could apply.

My home town of Massillon was close by. I felt I would have some ties when it came to recruiting. In fact, although I didn't get it, I had applied for the Kent State job the time before when it was open and I was an assistant at Michigan.

The selection committee was comprised of many of the same people I had talked to just a couple of years prior. Having known Mike a little bit from our Colorado ties and being from Ohio I thought I had a chance to at least be a finalist. We had a good interview and I got the job.

After I was named the head coach at Washington, Mike later came out as the A.D. and was my boss for another 15 years. Joe Kearney left Seattle as the Washington A.D. to go back to Michigan State. Joe offered me the chance to go with him as the head coach at Michigan State, but I told him we didn't want to move again. I liked it in Seattle. I told those who headed the selection committee that I didn't want to get involved in university politics, but I would appreciate it if they would give my old A.D. an interview. Mike went through the process and got the job.

Probably the hardest move for our children was the one from Colorado to Kent State — even though it was a great opportunity for their dad.

It was a difficult time for kids. It gave us all a lot of heartaches. Jeff was in the ninth grade, Jill in the eighth. That's a tough age for kids under the best of conditions. Jeff was the star football and baseball player and the captain of everything at the junior high level. All of a sudden he's faced with leaving for Ohio. He didn't want to move.

We told the kids that once you move you can never go back because it is never the same. But kids don't believe that, of course. Jeff was kind of resentful. So we told him that if he got a job at Kent and earned enough money, we'd let him fly back to Colorado during spring break. And he did.

It was February when the family moved. So just a couple of months later he went back to Boulder to stay with his "best" buddy. When he came back after spring break, Jeff was a completely different person. "Boy, have THEY changed," he said of his Boulder friends. His old girl friend had a new boy friend by that time. "They just aren't the same," he said.

Jill also went back the following summer and she too was ready to return to the family in Ohio in just a few days.

It was a good learning lesson for both kids.

chapter thirteen

*Coaching from a tower
gives me an overall view
of both the offense and defense*

I was the defensive coordinator at Florida State, Michigan and Colorado. Yet, the first thing I did when I became a head coach was to go out and hire a defensive coordinator.

I feel my job is to coach the coaches, who in turn coach the players. In my opinion, the No. 1 role of the head coach is to tie the whole package together. Get the coaches and the players going. Get the coordinators going. It's a matter of being the manager of the managers.

Many head coaches at the major college level take on a specific coaching responsibility. If the head coach is to coach a position or try to coordinate either the offense or defense, he will lose something that I don't want to lose in the overall scheme. How does he know what's going on at the other end of the field during practice?

It's the same as if I were to go on the road to recruit a certain area. Or if I were to coach a position. If

I did that, I wouldn't be able to see what is going on with the total picture. I don't want to lose control of the overall structure of the program.

That's why I became a "tower coach" from the outset of my head coaching career.

Most of the head coaches I worked with were offensive coaches. As their defensive coordinator I had much of the responsibility to run the defense without interference or input from the head coach. But I didn't want it to work that way when I was the head coach. I didn't have an attitude that I had to coordinate anything, but I want to know what's going on with the offense, defense and the kicking game.

I had a full complement of coaches when I was at Kent State. I didn't want to be on one end of the field and have a coach at the other end of the field swearing at a player or putting hands aggressively on a player or anything like that. Or making decisions on personnel that I didn't happen to see. Where I am, I can see everything that is going on. I can settle all the debates on personnel at the next morning's staff meeting and I can help make good decisions because I have seen the complete practice.

I'll never forget the time we were getting ready to play USC in 1981. Our scout squad, which runs the opposition plays in practice — to give our defense a look at what to expect the next Saturday — is made up mostly of freshmen. To a great extent, freshman who are being redshirted. None of the scout squad players are likely to see action in the upcoming game.

A freshman named Jacque Robinson was on the scout squad that year. He was pretending to be Marcus Allen, who was the Trojan tailback, while the scout team ran the USC plays against our defense.

I went to the staff meeting the next morning and said, "Hey, our freshman running back is looking better

Jacque Robinson: MVP of the Rose Bowl as a freshman.

than anybody we've got at the other end of the field with our offensive unit."

So we moved Jacque up to the varsity. He played a part in our beating the Trojans, ran well against Washington State the next week. In the Rose Bowl game against Iowa at the end of the season, Jacque was named the MVP of the Rose Bowl — as a freshman!

I want to be able to make those kinds of decisions. And you can't make them if you're down on the field, focused on one side of the ball.

I wouldn't think of going into a game without having a headset on and knowing what the offensive plan is. Not any more than I would be an offensive coordinator and turn over the defense to someone else and not know what's going on.

It's the same with the kicking game. I want to see all aspects of that too. I don't want to coordinate it. But I want to time the kickers from up in the tower and know that it's going the way I want. If I were involved with the offense or the defense, I could have a weak coach making bad decisions with the special teams and never know it.

That's why I wanted to be a tower coach. I wanted to be involved in everything, but not run everything with a 'hands-on' approach.

I had known some coaches who were tower coaches. Bear Bryant, of course, is the best known for having used that method. There are two things about being a tower coach that made it feel right for me.

First, if you are down on the field with either the offense or the defense, you can't know what is going on with the other side of the ball. Secondly, if an assistant coach is working with his position players, it would be easy to step in and say, "No, that's not the way I want it done. I want it done this way."

That could be perceived by the players as putting the assistant down. I want the players to have a total respect of their position coach.

When up in the tower observing, I take lots of notes. Then, in our daily staff meetings, I'll coach the coaches on what I want done. Then the assistants will coach the players.

We always film or video the practices. At the coaches meeting the next morning, when we critique the practice, everybody has input. That's when I can say to an assistant, "I don't want it done that way," or "That's not the way to coach that guy."

Once in a while, although it's rare, I might get mad and come down from the tower to straighten out something during a practice. But in most cases I try to put it in writing. I also try to avoid getting on a coach right after practice.

Sometimes I feel like doing so if I'm mad at them. But I've learned that I do the poorest job of coaching the players and coaches when I'm angry. A favorite phrase of Tex Winter, a former Washington basketball coach who is now an assistant with the Chicago Bulls, was that "for every minute you are angry you lose 60 seconds of happiness."

I've learned how not to say anything until after I've slept on it. It might not seem so serious the next day. And I can be more constructive in my criticism. I just do a better job. You can correct it in a way that the assistant can get something out of it.

I seldom have the time to bring a coach into my office individually to critique every mistake. I do, however, try to be as positive as I can because I want the coaches to be positive when they correct the players. And I certainly don't have the time to correct 150 football players one at a time. So you must learn to take constructive criticism in our program.

Our practices are well planned in advance and very detailed. Everything is scripted from start to finish. At any moment during the practice I can tell by the play being run down on the field exactly where we are.

With Paul 'Bear' Bryant, a true coaching legend.

I don't just sit up in that tower and say nothing. If things aren't going as well as I think they should, I can either come down or use a megaphone to get a point across.

I suppose some of my players, particularly the younger ones, may have been intimidated by my being up on a tower during practice. But it allows me to make objective decisions without personal involvement. More importantly, it gives me a clear view of the entire field and everything that is going on.

Although I never coached under him, I'm sure Bear Bryant had a great influence on my decision to be a tower coach.

When I was in college at Miami I played against his teams. Then he became "the guy" in college football — a real legend.

That's the way people looked at him. He had a great influence on the methods used by many coaches. When I was coaching at Florida State, it was just amazing. We'd go over and watch the Alabama practices. Or we'd listen to The Bear and his assistants speak at clinics on his ideas about speed and quickness and discipline. In those days, any young coach in his right mind should have been listening and had his note pad out.

Much later, after I was here at Washington, I remember the time my wife and I were on our way to attend a national coaching convention in Miami.

We were walking through the Miami airport and The Bear was approaching from the opposite direction. I said, "Hi, Coach." He said, "Don James! How are you?" We spoke for a minute or two.

When Carol and I walked away I said to her, "I think I've finally arrived in coaching. Bear Bryant knows who I am."

chapter fourteen

The media has created
a Don James image;
Is it the real me?

Because of all the articles that have been written by the media over the years, I'm afraid I now have an image of being someone other than myself.

Many of those articles have stressed the fact that Don James is basically a good guy who runs a clean program. But the writers often seem to feel compelled to add that he's also a person who doesn't drink, doesn't smoke, doesn't swear.

I don't want to disillusion those who believe everything they read in the newspapers, but all of those things aren't true. You should hear me after I make a bad golf shot or what I think is an incorrect call by an official.

I admit to being a Christian who is constantly attempting to be a better one. And I have much work to do on that account.

If you really want me to level with you, I look at the one issue of Playboy Magazine each fall with the Top Twenty college football prediction list. And I suppose I may have glanced at what was on some of the other pages in the magazine. As Carol says, "It's like National Geographic. Those are great pictures of places you're never going to visit."

I hope I'm more 'regular' and 'human' than some fans — and even some of my players — imagine me to be.

I never want to be associated with losing and I don't want to cheat to win. Before a game, when we're finished with the work and planning, I do worry and a lot of self-doubt creeps in. Sometimes you wonder how you're going to beat anybody, the opponents all look so good on film. Their players all look bigger and faster.

But I try to keep my negative feelings private. It would be dangerous for me to let the players know the doubt that I sometimes have. I usually go before them with a pretty positive attitude.

I suppose, because I try to prepare our team on a tight, regimented, disciplined schedule and in an organized way — and attempt to a keep my emotions under control — a lot of people view me as something I am not. I hope to be considered an understanding, caring person who is pleasant to be around, although most competitors are not much fun to be around the closer you get to a contest.

I always keep in mind the fact that coaches have an impact on the lives of youngsters. As a result, I am careful of what I might do in their sight. If someone saw me smoking a cigarette — which wouldn't happen since I don't smoke — but if I did, a youngster might think that meant it was okay for them to smoke. I think coaches should lead by example. Our young people don't need more sermons. They need more adults to look up to.

The reason I am a coach is because I wanted to model my life after my coaches. I've had great respect for them. Of all the courses I took in high school and college, I don't remember very many of my teachers or professors. But I remember all of my coaches. I remember everything about them and what they believed in.

Because of my success as a football coach, some people have said I am one of the more "powerful" people in the state. I'm not into being a power person. I don't want to be governor. I don't want any part of politics. I just want control of our football program from the standpoint of personnel. I don't want people telling me who to recruit, who to play or what plays to call. That's what I'm being paid to do.

I also realize that intercollegiate athletics is here for the athletes, not the coaches. We have an NCAA rule book an inch thick that governs everything we do. College presidents and athletic directors must work together to see that the programs have integrity and deserve to be on a college campus.

Some people may have thought I had political ambitions back in 1984 when both vice president George Bush and president Ronald Reagan made visits to Seattle and I introduced one and gave a memento to the other. I'll discuss that in more detail later.

Regarding my relationship with the players, just as I try to be a leader to the team as a whole, I expect the seniors to accept a role of leadership to their underclassman teammates. Every Thursday, for five weeks prior to the start of spring practice, I have a meeting with the seniors-to-be.

I want the seniors to be concerned about team leadership, not about getting an agent. So we discuss the NCAA agent rules. Among other things, I tell them the upcoming season should be their best year ever. Also, that no team can be great if the seniors aren't; that setting a good example for the others through effort, intensity, attitude and attendance is important.

The reason for the meetings is to get them all together to make them feel like this is their team and this is their most important season. They've got the most invested — three or four years — and they've got to play their best for the team to have a great season. This will be the year they should remember the most for the rest of their lives.

I do a little mini series on leadership. I've got some things I go through and just talk about what good leadership is and how they can concentrate and focus on being better leaders.

I also encourage them to come up with ideas that might help the football team be better. I encourage them to talk about every aspect of the team. The travel plans, uniforms, practices, anything. If they've got an idea they think will be an improvement in the way we do things, I want to know about it.

I don't want them to ever come in to the meeting thinking we should do less work. I don't want them to take the approach that it would be better if we didn't run as many wind sprints. But if there are one or two things that they all go back to the dorms and bitch about, this is the time to bring it up and how it could be done better.

I don't want to do that with the freshmen, sophomores or juniors. I do encourage anyone to come in if they've got a beef, complaint or idea, but this system helps the seniors-to-be open up a little more with me.

I've been doing this for a long time. I was never around any other coach who did it, but I've found it to be of value. And we've had a number of good suggestions from these meetings that we've incorporated. One idea is team meetings, every Friday night before each game, conducted by the captains without the coaches in attendance. That was Warren Moon's idea when he was our quarterback. They talk about the importance of the game, or whatever they want to talk about, and usually wind up very vocal and emotional. We've been doing that now for about 13 years because of Warren's suggestion. It gets them together before we bed check the evening prior to all games.

Sometimes the captains will ask for a team meeting, again without the coaches. They may want to get after their teammates if they don't feel everybody is giving 100 percent. The only restriction is that they can't have a meeting without me knowing about it. I want to know it's coming and I want to know what's on the agenda.

Also, when we play certain teams, I will designate players to make a brief comment or two about the game. Maybe we're playing Oregon and we've got some kids from Oregon on the team. They can talk about what the game means to them. We do that for the big games, the rival games.

Those are just some of the things that we do now because of suggestions from the players.

I'm not really buddy-buddy with my assistant coaches, let alone the players. When I was an assistant coach I always felt it was important for Carol and me to establish friendships outside the coaching staff. I had good friends on all the coaching staffs and enjoyed a lot of the guys — in fact, most all of them. But socially we tried to move out into the community and develop friendships. As coaches, we spend many hours together.

I'm sure some of the players think I'm standoffish. But decisions about personnel and position changes are always tough to make. And the more you can keep personalities out of that decision-making process, the better.

I have certainly never tried to present the image of being aloof to my players, but I suppose, because I have been on a tower much of the time while they were practicing, they didn't feel they knew me or were as close to me as they were to their position coaches.

A big lineman once told my wife, after he had finished his playing career, "How can a guy as big as me be so scared of a guy the size of your husband? I don't know why, but I was always scared to death of him."

With a Husky as the team mascot, everybody seemed to have fun with the promotion of me as the "Dawgfather".

Obviously, if I had to motivate people through fear and intimidation I'd be in a lot of trouble. I've heard the Woody Hayes and Bear Bryant stories. And there are a few other coaches who operate that way, but they are still living so I won't mention their names.

That's not the way I want to work. If I'm going to motivate a football team through fear and intimidation to get them to play, I've recruited the wrong group of guys and I don't want to have to coach that way.

Having the respect of the players is more important than having them as friends. I just don't think a team can play well, certainly not to its potential, unless they think we're doing a good job of coaching and thus have respect for us. I tell the coaches this every year. It's going to be hard to win a championship if our players don't think we're championship caliber coaches. If they think we're a bunch of dogs and don't know what direction we're going, if they think we're not very good teachers or coaches, we aren't going to win a championship.

When I was an assistant coach, I wanted my players to think I was the best defensive backfield coach in the country. They don't know all the coaches. I'm the only guy who coaches them. So I want them thinking that the things I'm doing and teaching — and the way they are playing — that I've got to be the best.

And I want my players today to believe the same thing about my assistants. You get this respect by helping players improve. They all want to be great players.

I'm aware of what the players say. A lot of times it's reported in the newspaper. One player said, "His practice sessions are so structured and time oriented that it makes a military operation seem haphazard." I took that as a compliment.

Others have said they would steal a glance up at me in the tower and wonder what I was really like. I read once where kicker Chuck Nelson said, "I think he did it on purpose. He liked to keep his distance. I think it must have made his decisions easier because there weren't personalities involved. He distanced himself from us so he could be more objective. I got to know him a lot better after I was done playing." Regardless of what they think, the door to my office is always open to the players. But you can't force them to come through the open door. I really try to work with the young men who need help, while I may not see a whole lot of the player who doesn't need much counseling.

I certainly don't ever walk by a player without speaking to him. I don't ignore them. But I'm in front of them so much. That's one thing I learned from other coaches. If you coach a group of guys for five years and you're in front of them, talking to them nearly every day, sometime they're going to say, "Here it comes again! We've heard this story every year for five years."

As a result, I've really tried to change up. I've tried not to be repetitive. I've been before Husky players for 16 years, before the game, after the game, at halftime, and my Thursday talks. And the guys who redshirt are here for five straight years. I deal with the seniors a good bit. And I deal with the captains more. When I speak to the team I always try to have information for them and avoid being redundant.

I've tried to project an image of being there. Two or three times a year I tell them, "I want you to come to me if and when you have problems. I want you to bring your problems to your position coach, to the coach who recruited you and to me."

I've told them about when I was in the service. I'd often come back to the barracks after a real hard, long day which was pretty productive, feeling good about things. Then, after sitting down on the cot, someone within earshot would start to complain. Before you knew it there would be a whole group of guys complaining and bitching. Before they started, you were feeling pretty good about the accomplishments of the day, even though it may have been a gruelling one. But the attitude of many was changed because of one or two guys telling everybody how you were being overworked, how hot it is, how wrong it is, how bad it is.

I learned a lot about group dynamics and the dynamics of leadership in the military. And I think it is also very important in the locker room. In a team concept, negative guys cause you a lot of headaches. And that's part of our evaluation when we go out to recruit a player. We don't want a bitcher, a complainer, a locker room lawyer. We want good positive kids who want to be the best they can be.

As I mentioned earlier, Chuck Nelson says he got to know me better after he got out of school. Some former players we hardly ever see. That even goes for some who still live in the Seattle area. Others have gotten very involved in various parts of the program.

We have a speakers' bureau. We bring in former players at fall camp to talk to our team about different subjects. The players can look up there and see a guy who is only a couple of years older than they are who is giving them some advice from his experiences.

We've had former and current pro players talk about agents — what to look out for, why you don't need one until you get drafted and what you should pay if you sign with one.

Others come back to talk about the job they are in. The guys really stress the fact that the primary thing is to get the degree. You may not work in your field of study, but that the degree is important. Some now have their own businesses and they talk about how they got started.

As I look back, a lot of the players I seemed to get the closest to were young men who grew up in homes with a single parent — usually a mother. They were more inclined to just pop into my office for brief visits. Maybe many of them wanted or needed more of a father influence.

I want them to know that I'm concerned about them. The thing I've tried to do too is tell them how proud I am of them, how much I respect them for their hard work in the program.

It's not an easy thing to be a major college football player — or a coach.

chapter fifteen

*Recalling the most
memorable games against
cross-state rival WSU*

Our annual game against Washington State is
known as the Apple Cup. It's one of the few games that
WSU sells out, so we obviously take a bunch of our fans
with us when it's played over there. And that's somewhat surprising since it's about a six-hour drive. Plus
you have mountain passes to contend with, and you can
get a lot of snow on the passes late in the fall.

We beat them in the first seven meetings after I became the head coach and through the 1990 season had a
12-4 record against the Cougars.

But none of the games has been more exciting than
my first in 1975. And the player who created most of
the excitement that day was a freshman wide receiver
named Robert "Spider" Gaines.

Spider, who came from Oakland, California, was on
our recruiting list from the outset. He came primarily
to play football, although he was an outstanding track
man.

Robert 'Spider' Gaines lettered as a freshman after just
seven minutes of playing time.

Our rule on a scholarship player being on the track or baseball team is that he must participate in spring football his first year. If he plays a spring sport, he must double up. In his following years, an athlete can spend all spring with track or baseball if he wants to.

Most of them don't want to miss out on spring ball and let somebody bypass them on the depth chart, however. So if they want to double up, they try to work at both sports while not missing any more of spring practice than absolutely necessary.

Spider was an outstanding hurdler. He advanced all the way to the Olympic Trial finals in 1976 as a 19-year old sophomore. His junior year he was ranked 5th in the United States and 8th in the world as a 110-meter hurdler.

He started his freshman year on the scout squad. Before moving Spider up to the varsity I had been up in the tower with my stopwatch, timing him while he was rushing our punter during some drills.

I felt he might be able to block some punts. With his speed, I thought he could come from the corner and block punts quicker than they could get them off. I went to him and asked him what he thought. Most receivers aren't too keen about trying to block punts. But, since he was a freshman and not playing, he wanted to give it a try.

The first time we got him in a game, the sixth of the season, was against Stanford. He blocked two punts in that one game and both of them were converted into touchdowns. He drove people nuts from then on.

In addition to those two, in just seven minutes of playing time for the entire season, Spider blocked a field goal attempt against Oregon State the following week; deflected a field goal against UCLA the next week; and two weeks later trapped the USC punter in the end zone for a safety that provided the margin of victory against the Trojans.

Then came the Washington State game in which he caught three TD passes, including a 78-yarder on the game's final play to win the game for us 28-27.

That was the wildest finish in which I've ever been involved. Late in the game, the Cougars were up 13 points and had the ball inside our five-yard line. Yet on fourth down they were worried about trying a field goal — which would have put the game completely out of reach — for fear Spider might block it and run it back 95 yards for a touchdown.

So, they called time out. WSU Coach Jim Sweeney wanted to run the ball. That would have been the smart thing to do. But his players were a little greedy. They wanted to run a fake dive and what we call a fire pass. That's a quick look-in pass to the tight end over the middle after first faking the ball to the dive back.

But we had a call on that put Al Burleson, our weak safety, right into the zone of their tight end. And Al intercepted the pass and ran it back 97 yards for a touchdown.

Now we were only down by six points. We would have been down two touchdowns and a field goal if they had kicked one, or down two touchdowns with 97 yards to go if they had just run it into the line. Instead, they called the worst possible play for them and the best for us. Now we were down just six points with a couple of minutes left to play.

We had some time outs left, so we didn't try an onside kick. We kicked it deep, which probably surprised a lot of people. But I figured they would play it pretty conservatively after what had happened on that pass. So I didn't seriously consider an onside kick. If we had done that, and didn't recover the ball, we would have put them in field goal range in a hurry. The way it was, we had them deep enough that they weren't going to try anything fancy. We just ganged up against the run and called time out after each play. We stopped them in three plays and they had to punt.

Warren Moon was our quarterback. He then threw a couple of passes. One was a long one that was tipped by Scott Phillips and Spider reached in, picked it right off the shoulder pads of one of the Washington State defensive backs and ran it in for a touchdown. We kicked the extra point and won it, 28-27.

The game was played in Seattle. But by the time all that happened the stadium was almost empty. It was cold and wet and the Cougars thought they had the game won. Their band had already started a snake dance all around the stadium.

Our fans figured it was all over, too. They had headed for the exits. For that matter, I also thought it was over. They should have won it. But they didn't.

There were a lot of stories about people who heard the noise once they left the stadium. Some tried to get back in, some listened on the radio. It was wild.

We had some excitement of a different kind in the most recent game this past season over at WSU. We were out on the field for our pre-game workout when we saw them completely clearing one section of the stands. One of the game administrators from WSU came up to me and said they'd had a bomb scare and that they were going to clear this one section.

He came back before we completed our workout and said they had now decided to clear the field of both teams. We went back into the locker room and just waited and waited. We didn't know when — or if — the game was going to start.

We had one false alarm. They brought us out, but then somebody higher up said, "No, we're not ready to have the teams out here yet," So back we went again.

They did locate a makeshift bomb. It was some kind of a student prank. During the search they asked all the people in the stadium to look under their seat to see if they could find something that resembled a bomb. Most people were anxious to look — if they hadn't already done so.

They tried to move the students out of their section, but the kids had come so early in order to get a decent seat that they weren't about to move willingly.

We finally got the game underway about 45 minutes late.

Our relationship with Washington State has generally been good. One exception occurred soon after the completion of my first season in Seattle. Joe Steele, a top local area recruit, had committed to us early because he had decided he didn't want to go through the hassle of recruiting.

I had gone to the office early the morning Joe announced his intention. Carol got a phone call at home. It was from Jackie Sherrill, who had just gotten the head coaching job at Washington State.

Carol congratulated Jackie on getting the job and told him I had left for the office. But he cut her off in mid-sentence and said, "Just because your husband beat USC and UCLA this year, he thinks he's a Knight on a white horse. And I want to tell you he's cheating real bad on recruiting."

Carol said he went on and on and jumped all over her about Joe Steele committing early. Carol told him that if he had something to say he should say it to me, not her. He never did do that. The truth is that Joe Steele wasn't about to go to Washington State, anyway. He was a good student and could have gone anywhere in the country.

I heard that a year later, after Sherrill left Washington State and took the Pittsburgh job, that he did the same thing to Joe Paterno's wife.

Now Jackie seems to be off to a similar start with his new job at Mississippi State.

chapter sixteen

*Bowl game preparation;
and a recap of our
'Big One' against Michigan*

In many respects, because of the layoff after the conclusion of the regular season, preparing a team for a bowl game is just like getting ready for a brand new, one-game season.

And that problem is compounded by the fact that in a bowl game you're always matched against a team that has had an exceptional year. That means it's going to be one of the toughest opponents of the season.

As a result, I'm proud of the 9-3 bowl record we have amassed in our 12 bowl games at the University of Washington.

A lot of coaches, for some reason, go to the bowl site late. Many of them arrive the day after Christmas for a January 1 game that is just one week away.

That would bother me. First of all, it takes a day or two to settle in and be comfortable with the new surroundings at the hotel and the practice facility. There are also a myriad of distractions to deal with while trying to make your final preparations.

Each bowl has a committee that wants to show off the area's hospitality. They organize a lot of very nice things for the players to do. At the Rose Bowl that means a visit to Knottsberry Farm, Disneyland and the Universal Studio tour among other thing.

No matter what bowl you go to, there's lots of social life. The committee will even occasionally schedule a dance, bringing in local girls. If a team doesn't arrive until after Christmas, the players are going deep sea fishing, visiting amusement parks, having outdoor steak fries and things like that for three or four days. That leaves practically no time at all to properly prepare for the game.

After being entertained to death, the players are tired. They've been on their feet all day yet still haven't really buckled down to practice.

So instead of staying in Seattle where the weather might prevent us from practicing outdoors, I prefer going to the bowl site an extra week early. We also do not have an indoor practice facility.

That decision is made even easier because the dorms are closed as soon as final exams are over. As a result, since we still have to house and feed the guys, why not go where the sun is shining and house and feed them there. That way we can get all the fun activities done the first week and concentrate on winning the game the second week.

During that first week we have the most carefree bunch of kids you've ever seen. There's lots of laughter, whooping and hollering. They just have fun — work hard and play hard. We conclude that first week with a big family dinner on Christmas Eve. Each table of ten has its own turkey with all the trimmings.

After dinner we have team entertainment. Each class puts on some skits, musical numbers, things like that. Then we give them their bowl watches and whatever other gifts there are before excusing them until the 26th.

When they come back, there is a change in attitude that is just like night and day. For the last week the players are ready to get down to work and think about football. Besides, by that time they're running a little short of cash so they can start to focus on the opponent.

The captains bed check two nights prior to the game and we, the coaches, bed check the night before the game. And that's the only two nights of bed check we have for the entire two weeks.

If there are going to be any problems, they are going to surface the first couple of days after we arrive. The players are excited about getting to the bowl site and having fun. But they soon realize that they're going to have to pay the price if they party too much the night before as we hold morning workouts.

The importance of going to the bowl site early also is apparent when it comes to recruiting. The vast majority of the high school athletes that we have recruited think in terms of (1) Where will I be given the chance to play from early in my career; (2) Where can I go to be with a winner that goes to a bowl game almost every year and also appears on TV a lot; and (3) Where can I get a good education.

I say it in that order because I must admit that's probably the order in the minds of most recruits. Their parents might well put education first instead of third. I think an opportunity to play and an opportunity to have success — which translates into post-season play and television exposure — is very vital in the decision-making process for a recruit. So we sell it. We keep the recruits up to date on what we've done.

The interesting thing about recruiting is we're selling the player's future and our past. We're trying to get the recruit to come and play for us because this is what we've done before. We've won 'x' number of games; we've won 'x' number of bowl games; and we've projected where he can fit into our situation to keep the program successful.

Regarding preparation of the team for a bowl game, there appears to be a lot of things we do differently from other coaches.

First of all, I don't want the bowl experience to be like a Marine boot camp. I don't want it to be like fall camp or spring practice. I want the players to feel as though it's a reward for having had a good season. I think that is the key approach.

After the layoff at the end of the regular season, it would be easy to bring a team back and work them so hard and get them beat up to the point where they would become angry at the coaches rather than the opponents. I'd rather have them ready to play and have respect for the opponent. That's one premise.

We give the players a lot of flexibility and freedom. We also let the players get involved with the bowl gifts. We take the dollar limit the NCAA allows and the players get involved in picking the things they want, whether they are sweats or bags, jackets, whatever. If we win a championship and they get a ring, the players even get involved in its design.

As a result, I think the players feel a real part of the process. I think they're pleased with the trip and they're ready to play. We give them enough of a free reign so they can go out and enjoy the community we're in. We even let them pick the events and the number of events that are offered. There is a lot of player involvement.

On the years that we get invited to the Rose Bowl or some other game on January 1st, there is about a month from the end of the regular season until the 17th or 18th of December when we leave for the bowl site.

We only have a very few practices during that month. Our last game this past year was against Washington State on the 17th of November. We went down to LA on the 18th of December. The four days before we left we had two practices in sweats and two in full pads.

In those other three plus weeks we encouraged the people who handle the ball to handle it, but there was nothing structured. We want them to get caught up on their academics and we asked them to lift weights a couple of days each week. But there was nothing they really had to do. The players need a rest after the regular season. It's been a long grind for them. The smart ones are going to work out and stay in shape.

Once we know who we are playing, we call and institute a trade agreement on film. In most cases, we agree to trade all 11 game films with our bowl opponent.

Our assistant coaches usually pick the five games they really want to study and the grad assistants break those films down and get them into the computerized scouting report form.

Each coach will also take film and individually study it. But, at the same time, we are also doing prospect evaluation and getting started on recruiting.

When we come back and start practices we know pretty much what basic offensive and defensive formations our bowl opponent is going to use. Of course we don't know the exact plays they're going to run. Nor have we made that decision for ourselves yet either.

So we just practice against our opponent's basic plays for the first couple of days. Each day after that we start to add a little more game plan and usually in five or six days we have the game plan finished.

There is not the urgency you have during the regular season. The bowls are the fun part of football. I'd hate to see them go by the wayside in favor of a playoff.

It is true that Washington had not been to a bowl game for 11 years before I got here. But you must remember that the long-time rule for the Pac-10 was Rose Bowl or nothing. The league had a lot of good bowl teams. But if they weren't the league champion and went to the Rose Bowl they stayed home.

As I covered earlier, my first two teams had an even .500 record. Then we started the 1977 season with just one victory and three defeats. When you've got that kind of record, and it looks like it might be the end of your career, and in a matter of a few short weeks you become a Rose Bowl winner, the "Cinderella team" tag does seem to fit.

But I also had the feeling that our fans were beginning to believe, "Maybe this new staff knows what they're talking about. Maybe they will be able to coach football at this university."

The team had gained a lot of confidence and they'd played some good football teams. The players felt they had a legitimate chance to prove something. But we were at least a two touchdown underdog going into the Rose Bowl game against Michigan.

Although the players worked hard and prepared well, we didn't look especially good at times in practice. A couple of days while preparing for the game it really rained hard. We were working out at a junior college and their practice field became a sea of mud.

But, rather than call things off, we practiced on the black top parking lot at the junior college for a couple of days. I know we were in pads one day. The practice field was far from dry, but after a couple of days we moved the defense back onto it to work on goal line defenses.

Jim Mora's brother worked down in the LA area. That particular day he came out to watch us. I don't know if we could totally blame things on the muddy field, but that day our No. 1 defense couldn't stop the scout squad offense. It got so bad and I got so angry that I left in disgust and went back to the parking lot to watch the offense work out.

Mora's brother went back to his office and told everybody to "bet all the money you've got on Michigan because that Washington defense couldn't stop a decent high school team." We did look bad that day.

But, when game day arrived, we had every psychological advantage in the world. The fact that we were 7 and 4 had the papers saying we had backed into the Rose Bowl, that we were not all that good.

Here was Michigan, coming out with this great team and heavy favorites. The media was kind of beating us up during the weeks leading up to the game, while at the same time telling Michigan how good they were.

So what happened? We were up 17-0 at halftime and 27-7 going into the fourth quarter. They did score two fourth quarter touchdowns to close it to 27-20 and were on another drive. But Michael Jackson, our fine linebacker, made a key interception to stop that drive. In fact, we had two interceptions in the fourth quarter, the other by Nesby Glasgow. Those were very critical to our cause. Once we got ahead they had to go to the pass.

Rick Leach was their quarterback. And though they gained 239 yards passing, that was not normally their No. 1 offensive weapon. Warren Moon had 12 completions of 23 attempts, gaining 188 yards for us. He then signed with the Canadian League before the NFL draft.

A couple of amusing things stick out in my mind from that game. Ray Door had told his wife Karen, "If we somehow get ahead at any time during the game, I want you to take a picture of the scoreboard." Well, we scored first and she took the picture. When they got the prints back, it showed clear as anything: "Michigan 6, Washington 0."

Everybody was so sure Michigan was going to win they even credited the Wolverines with our first touchdown.

After the game, when I was walking out through the tunnel, somebody was carrying a sign that said, "Michigan 14, Custer 0".

Pass interceptions by
Michael Jackson (above)
and Nesby Glasgow
(right) helped preserve
our victory over
Michigan in the 1978
Rose Bowl.

That Rose Bowl got us going and gave us a good recruiting base. And we had done well recruiting early. What we had to do then was prove it was not a one time deal. That we could stay a contender and that we were not going to remain a Cinderella team.

chapter seventeen

*A Sun Bowl win over Texas
went a long way toward proving
that we were back and for real*

Although we had a decent year in 1978 — we tied for second in the Pac-10 standings with league losses only to UCLA and USC — we didn't get a bowl bid.

But, after the next season, we were invited to the Sun Bowl to play a great opponent in Texas.

I always thought they should call that the "Fun Bowl". The committee really worked hard at seeing that everybody had a good time.

Soon after we got to El Paso they took both teams to a big cookout dinner, then later in the week to a Sheriff's Posse breakfast.

One of the features at the cookout was a talent show contest where a few players from our team and some from Texas would get up and entertain.

We had a great two-man combo. Antwaine Richardson, a linebacker, was the drummer and Tom Porras, our quarterback, was the guitarist and singer. They

Antowaine Richardson
"Remember me? I'm the
drummer."

Tom Porras
Quarterback, guitarist,
singer,
And still playing pro ball
in Canada.

were really good. Tom is still playing football in Canada and Antwaine sings professionally.

We won the talent contest hands down. The Texas players were no match. After the talent show, the Texas quarterback said to Antwaine, "You may have won the talent show, but we'll win the game."

Well, on the last play of the game, when Texas was trying desperately to throw a 'Hail Mary' pass while trailing 14-7, Antwaine sacked that quarterback. While he's on top of the guy and got him pinned down, Antwaine says to him, "Remember me. I'm the drummer."

After knocking off Michigan in the Rose Bowl, I think that topping Texas two seasons later really helped solidify our program and showed people that we were for real.

We may have had the same advantage in that Sun Bowl as we had in the Rose Bowl game against Michigan. I'm not sure Texas was as excited about being there as we were. The Longhorns had also been in the Sun Bowl the year before and had beaten Maryland real bad. They may not have been all that excited about being back.

In fact, one of their players said to one of ours, "We want to get some points up there early so our backups can play. They didn't get to play too much this year." It was as if he was saying we weren't a very worthy opponent and they were anxious to get the second team in the game.

Texas, which was coached by Fred Akers, had one of the best defenses we ever played against. The game was one of the most fiercely contested, had the most big hits of any game I've ever seen. Both teams were just cracking people. A lot of coaches around the country who saw that game requested the film so they could show their players how defense should be played. They were obviously impressed with the aggressiveness of the players.

Although it was tough, hard-fought, hard-hitting and aggressive, it was a clean, well-played game.

All the points were scored in the second quarter. We got two touchdowns and they scored one. I mentioned how good their defense was. They held us to 165 yards of total offense.

Tom Flick was our other quarterback. He was a local kid from here in Bellevue. This was the first season when he had a chance to start and play. The next year he took us back to the Rose Bowl.

The year before, when we didn't go to a bowl game, Tom Porras was at quarterback. He played some the next year before Flick took over. In that Sun Bowl game, we had a freshman wide receiver named Paul Skansi. He caught five passes from Flick, was named the Sun Bowl MVP and is still playing for the Seattle Seahawks. But that was about our entire offense.

One other standout player on that team was cornerback Mark Lee. He's still playing with Green Bay. Mark was a good cover guy and an excellent punt returner.

A couple of incidents in connection with the Sun Bowl games we've played in stand out in my memory as much as the games.

The first one occurred just before the start of that game against Texas. The issue was what game balls would be used.

We had an equipment man assigned to us from UTEP where we worked out. He said, "Coach, you wait and see, they won't let you use your footballs. The officials are going to use the balls given to them by the bowl committee."

No quarterback wants to use a brand new football. They like a ball they have thrown some — a ball that is scuffed up a little. I told the equipment man we weren't going to want to use brand new balls. But he said again, "You wait a and see."

Paul Skansi: MVP at the Sun Bowl as a freshman.

After being on the field to warm up for the game, we were on our way back to the dressing room when one of the officials stopped me and said, "We aren't going to use your balls in the game because you didn't get them to us within the prescribed time."

I said, "What do you mean. You knew where our equipment room has been all week. We didn't know where to find you. We've had our balls ready all week but didn't know where you were. And you say you're not going to use our balls."

"No sir, we aren't," the ref answered. "You didn't get them to us on time and they haven't been checked out." "Well, then," I answered, "I'll tell you what. We're not going to play the game. We're just going to sit in the dressing room. I don't know what time the game is supposed to start, but if we don't get to use our balls we're not going to play."

The rule says that each team can furnish their own balls, thus allowing them to use the brand they like. There are three brands — Rawlings, Spaulding and Wilson — that are all acceptable under the NCAA rules. That's so the home team can't dictate which ball you use. After all, quarterbacks like to use the brand they always practice throwing.

The rule says the balls "shall be new or slightly used." We've had people in our league submit balls that are just too beat up. If it's more than slightly used the quarterback likes it because he'll get a better grip. And, if it is really old and has turned into a pumpkin, the kickers like those.

Each team is supposed to submit six balls to the officials. That gives them three for your ball boy on each side of the field. Prior to the game, the officials check to make sure the balls have the proper air pressure. The officials then keep them until just before the kickoff.

On that subject, we've had some people in our league who have deflated the balls after they had been checked. Our ball boy on the opponents side of the field saw them let some of the air out of the balls after the game started.

Quarterbacks don't like the required 13 pounds pressure if they can get away with a little less and thus get a better grip.

Anyway, in that Sun Bowl game, one of the host committee members named John Folmer saw me arguing with the ref and realized there was a rather heated discussion going on. He came down out of the press box and asked the official what was going on. Then he made the official take our balls and get them checked so the game could start. Folmer knew I meant what I had said.

We had an interesting thing on that same subject at our Rose Bowl game this last January against Iowa. At the end of the regular season, Charlie Finley, the ex-major league baseball team owner who at one time came up with the idea of an orange baseball for night games, developed a football that had inverted dimples.

The company manufacturing them for him sent us some balls to try out. Our quarterbacks liked them, but our kickers didn't. The quarterback liked the grip. I think the kickers missed one try in practice and decided it was the fault of the dimples. Anyway, they didn't want to use them.

So we gave the officials four balls with the inverted dimples and two of the regular kind. Since we provide our own ball boys, we orchestrated a situation where the ball boys were to throw in the inverted dimple ball on all but fourth down or when we were going to try a field goal or extra point kick. Each ball boy had two with the new dimples and one for the kickers.

A lot of people aren't yet familiar with the inverted dimple ball, although it will probably be more widely used in another season or two. Finley says he came up with the idea — although somebody else is challenging

him and says it was their invention. Anyway, Finley is
marketing it through Wilson, so Wilson made the balls.

If you just glance at it, you can't tell the difference.
You really have to study it. It's kind of like the difference in the alignment of the dimples on the different
makes of golf balls. The argument, like that for various
golf balls, is that it's supposed to go straighter and far-
ther — and give the quarterback a better grip.

But back to the other incident connected with one
of our trips to the Sun Bowl. In the first one, I almost
went on strike because we weren't going to be allowed
to use our game balls.

The second one was a strike of sorts by our players
a few days before we left for our Sun Bowl game
against Alabama following the 1986 season.

One player — I guess he was the "locker room lawyer" type — tried to talk the rest of the players into going on strike. The complaint, believe it or not, was that
I was practicing them so much they didn't have enough
time to study.

We had set out the practice schedule for the days
prior to leaving Seattle. Except for a handful of guys,
the players were all done with their final exams. I
think there were two players who still had a final to
take before we went to the bowl site.

We have never, ever considered having a player
practice rather than go to class — let alone having practice interfere with taking a final.

But, this player got in the locker room and started
telling the others that they were being worked too hard
— that they didn't have enough time to study. Of
course he was a guy who didn't know the meaning of
the word study. In fact, he didn't last much longer
before he flunked out.

Anyway, he created enough interest that the captains came over to see me. They caught me by complete
surprise. They told me the team wasn't going to
practice.

That didn't turn out to be true. Most of the players were already dressed and out on the field. I told the captains to go back in the locker room and tell them that I want to meet, in the team meeting room, with anyone who didn't want to practice.

Most of the guys were afraid to even consider doing something like that. But a few of them were there when I arrived. There were two or three players in that group that bothered me. One was a guy who had decided to quit, but we had let him return and we had given him his scholarship back. He should never have considered something like that.

Secondly, the captains should never have let it happen. I thought it was very poor leadership on their part. I got a little angry. So I let them know that it was fine if anyone didn't want to practice, they didn't have to practice.

Of course I also let them know that they could also stay home from the bowl game. We weren't going to take them with us, and it didn't matter if they were a sub, a starter or a captain.

Needless to say, the "strike" never really got started.

chapter eighteen

Oklahoma: A big win! and a look back at the other bowl games

Each of the 12 bowl games has been important to maintaining our program at the University of Washington.

The first one, the Rose Bowl triumph over Michigan in our third year, the win over Texas in the Sun Bowl and the 28-17 victory over Oklahoma in the Orange Bowl following the 1984 season to cap an 11-1 record, probably did the most to establish our credibility.

The game against Texas started a string of nine straight bowl appearances for us.

The next two years we returned to the Rose Bowl, losing a rematch to Michigan following the 1980 season but shutting out Iowa, 28-0, to finish 10-2 the next year.

So, from 1977 to '81 we had a pretty good run of success for a new program. Three Rose Bowls and a Sun Bowl.

Now we've been to 12 bowl games in the last 14 seasons, missing only after 1978 and '88. Maybe I'd better retire before the 1998 season, although if we only miss

Paul Sicuro, our starting quarterback against Oklahoma
in the Orange Bowl is now a physician.

being selected for a bowl game just once every 10 years I think that would be pretty darn good.

After those back-to-back Rose Bowl games came two Aloha Bowl games in Hawaii. Both were very close games. We beat Maryland in '82, 21-20, but were edged by Penn State the next year, 13-10.

Then came the Oklahoma game in the Orange Bowl. The Sooners had a fine team, especially on defense with linebacker Brian Bosworth and middle guard Tony Cassillas.

Our offensive staff did a great job of game planning. We had a trap scheme for Cassillas that was very successful.

Paul Sicuro started at quarterback for us, then Hugh Millen came in. Hugh is still playing pro ball. Sicuro is a doctor.

Steve Sewell was OU's top rusher. He's still with the Denver Broncos. That was a big year and a prestigious victory for our program.

At that point we had played in seven bowl games in eight years. And, among the victories were wins over Michigan in the Rose Bowl, Texas in the Sun Bowl and Oklahoma in the Orange Bowl. That really gave us credibility.

Our only loss that season was to USC, a loss that kept us out of another Rose Bowl. But, when the Trojans lost in the Rose Bowl, we had high hopes that one of the wire service polls would pick us No. 1 after beating a very good Oklahoma team. BYU was named No. 1, however, although most people didn't feel they had played as tough a schedule as we had.

We had beaten Michigan at Ann Arbor and a good Houston team prior to our Pac-10 schedule. They were certainly both challenging opponents.

But BYU was unbeaten for the year and we wound up No. 2 in both polls.

In 1985 we met Colorado in the Freedom Bowl. That wasn't one of our better years. We were 6 and 5 on the regular season and salvaged a 7 and 5 record with a 20-17 win over the Buffaloes in the bowl game.

I don't think our fans were too upset with our record, however. We had to play a lot of young kids that year. We lost all of a great defense from the year before.

That was Bill McCartney's first bowl game at Colorado. Fred Cassotti was about the only guy in the athletic department who had been there when I coached at Colorado. That was a fun experience for me because Eddie and Jean Crowder and some of the others we were close to in Boulder came for the game.

We went back to the Sun Bowl in 1986 to play Alabama. Although we got beat we had an improved regular season. We went into the bowl game with an 8-2-1 record.

Our two losses were to USC and Arizona State and the tie was with UCLA. But we beat Ohio State and BYU and our other league opponents.

I thought this was one of our best teams physically, but we just didn't win as many games as I thought we might. We beat Ohio State, 40-7, and they later beat Texas A&M in the Cotton Bowl.

In our second game that year, we got BYU by a 52-21 score. We owed them a payback since they had taken the national championship away from us two years before. We opened up that game by giving up a kickoff return for a touchdown to put BYU ahead. I don't know why it was in there, but I'll never forget that there was an article in the paper the week of that game saying that a Don James coached team had never given up a touchdown from a kickoff return.

But our kids really got after them and built up a 32 to 7 halftime lead.

We certainly learned something from that Alabama game. We realized that we needed more speed instead of size after dealing with Cornelius Bennett and trying to catch Bobby Humphries.

We went into that Alabama game with a lot of guys hurt. I don't think I've ever gone into a game with so many guys banged up. If the game had been two or three weeks later we might have been in better shape. Moe Hill, our top receiver, who is now playing for New Orleans, had dislocated his elbow in the last regular season game.

Our starting fullback had a separated shoulder, and a first string tackle broke a bone in his hand just before the game. Another starter had a badly sprained ankle.

But they beat us. Perkins had a good team. And he took off for Tampa Bay right after that game.

We stayed with them for a half and trailed by just a point a 7-6.

That bowl game was followed by a 24-12 victory over Tulane in the Independence Bowl in 1987.

We were happy to be invited, but the local press thought it was a big comedown. It might have been, but those bowl organizers work just as hard at trying to put on a quality event as the Rose and Orange Bowl people.

The next year, Oregon was invited to the same bowl, after not having been to any bowl for years and years. Unlike our situation the year before, the press made it sound like it was the greatest thing that ever happened to a team from the Northwest.

I guess it all depends on the expectations of your fans.

All the bowl committees are wonderful and work so hard that it bothers me when any bowl is put down.

The wolves howled when we didn't get a bowl invitational following a 6-5 season in 1988. But we returned to the Freedom Bowl in 1989 for a game against Florida.

Jim Murray, the popular sports columnist for the Los Angeles Times, wrote an extremely flattering article about me prior to that game.

It was titled, "This coach stands out in a crowd of his peers."

Murray wrote: "The Freedom Bowl.

1.   A football game played annually in Shreveport. Or possibly Memphis.
2.   The tabloid name given to what's happening in Eastern Europe today.
3.   A new 32-lane facility in Downey where the last 300 game was rolled. Or,
4.   A place where you go to watch the Easter Sunrise Service.

"Actually, the answer is none of the above. The Freedom Bowl is a football game alright and a good one. It's played right down the road from the Rose Bowl but it's not to be confused with the Rose, Super, Sugar or even the Gator, Copper or Peach Bowls. It's more like the John Hancock Bowl or even the Hall of Fame or Liberty Bowls. Made for television.

"It's held in Anaheim. Which didn't want to be left out of the bowl picture altogether. No self-respecting community should be without one this time of year. There are 22 of them sanctioned by the NCAA with some 2,000 players involved, but of course the schools persist in resisting a national collegiate playoff. It would keep too many athletes out of the classroom they say — with a perfectly straight face.

"Anaheim started putting together a bowl of its very own eight years ago. For the most novel of reasons. A colleague, John Hall, writing in another paper, noticed glumly, that two of the nation's outstanding college backs — Marcus Allen and Herschel Walker — had no bowl game to go to that year. He suggested they contrive one for them.

"I suppose that's as good a reason for having a bowl game as any. I mean, not having a Marcus Allen or a Herschel Walker on your holiday screen is a cultural deprivation akin to not having a TaluceLetrec in the master bath. So they strung together the Freedom Bowl — too late, as it happened, for Marcus or Herschel — but just in time for the likes of Gaston Green, Chris Chandler, Chuck Long and a host of other stars who were to not get an otherwise available opportunity to be showcased in a bowl game.

"They probably should call it the Statue of Liberty Bowl, a refuge for the huddled masses yearning to run free.

"It's practically an institution now. The grandchild of them all. They've had five of them. But what makes this year's renewal interesting is not the players, it's a coach.

"It comes as a surprise to no student of the game that Don James, the University of Washington coach, has won more games in the Pacific 10 — or the conference's various other names — than any coach in history. More than the storied Howard Jones. More than Pop Warner, John McKay, Red Sanders or Pappy Waldorf. Shortly, he will have won more games, period, than any Pacific Coast coach ever.

"He has won more football games at Washington than Knute Rockne did at Notre Dame. He's no secret to the profession. His fellow coaches elected him president of the American Football Coaches Association.

"In another era, he'd probably have been known as 'The Fox' or be called 'Bo' or 'Bear' or even 'Pop' or 'Hurry Up'. He's not even 'Dr. J'. Hardly, anyone even calls him Mr. James.

"James brings a new meaning to the term low profile. James is, like his teams, controlled, disciplined, programmed. But not robotized. In the 1978 Rose Bowl, James' Washington team won the game because, late in the action with the ball on its own 24 yard line, fourth down and a bundle, his team went for it. And made it.

"His teams can be adventurous but seldom rash. They never panic. They lose, but not by much. Alabama beat him 52-0, the fifth game he coached at Washington. Three years later, the score of an Alabama-Washington game was 20-17.

"James' record is remarkable when you consider the University of Washington is not your basic football factory. Coaches leave the northwest in droves to coach in Texas, Florida and California. Players historically opt for the Northwest only if they have exhausted other options. 'If USC or Notre Dame wants a kid I don't get him,' James concedes.

"Recruiting has been further complicated with the addition of Arizona and Arizona State to the conference. Seattle is a long way from the Sun Belt. The gag goes, "Washington: First in war, first in peace and last in recruiting." None of this bothers Coach James who is as stable a fixture in Seattle as the Space Needle and who is known as "Home, James" because of his team's penchant for winning on its own field.

"In the Freedom Bowl Saturday at Anaheim Stadium, James meets a Florida team that is, like his, a highly underrated team that lost one game by five points, one by three and another two by a touchdown. All of this, after losing its head coach to a scandal.

"James' team lost to Rose Bowl-bound USC by a touchdown and to all-world Colorado, the nation's No. 1 team, 45-28. Washington lost to Arizona State by two points and Arizona by three.

"You may have a little trouble picking out Don James Saturday. He won't be pulling any yard markers out of the ground and hurling them at the officials; he won't be slamming his hat onto the turf while screaming at his players; he won't pace up and down the sideline like a caged leopard. He'll be hard to tell from the guy who is there to pick up the towels.

"After the game he won't keep the locker room door closed. It'll be hard to tell by looking at him whether he won or lost. Either way, it won't be by much."

As it turned out, we won the game rather handily, 34-7.

Murray sent me a copy of the column. On the bottom he wrote a note: "For Don James, the Dean. What a coach should be."

I know Florida was in transition with the coach leaving and all, but our kids acted like it was the first game of the rest of their life. They prepared well and that was the beginning of a real turnaround for our program.

chapter nineteen

One of the most important
factors in my life
is a close-knit family

After a rather meager beginning, I have been blessed with much in my life. No. 1, and something money can't buy, is a close-knit family. My family means a great deal to me.

I happen to think that the family unit can be the key to happiness and a satisfying life.

Most of the problems we have in the world today are people problems. Oh, we have storms, volcanos and other natural disasters, but basically our major problems are people problems.

What we have are too many people who don't want to be parents. There are too many who are not willing to make the sacrifices necessary to be good parents. And too many who have kids who are unwanted from the beginning.

It's the neglected kids who are experiencing the most problems. When you look at troubled youth and dig into their background, it many times starts with poor or indifferent parenting. Not always, but to even

This 1985 picture is missing a son-in-law and four grandchildren from today's total family.

Back row, from left: Son-in-law and UW assistant coach Jeff Woodruff, daughter Jeni, Carol and son Jeff.

Front, from left, daughter Jill, her son Jared, daughter-in-law Rosemary and her son Jeffrey.

have a chance, a youngster has to have parents who are there for them and willing to spend the time.

As I said, my family is important to me, yet at the same time I felt the necessity to be fully dedicated to my job. First of all, if I hadn't had a wife like Carol I'd no doubt have a family problem. She was always able to carry the heavy load in raising the kids during the fall football season. No question about it. You can imagine what our house would have been like if I worked the hours I do and Carol had a job outside the home and was not there for the children.

Don't label me a male chauvinist who thinks a woman's place is only in the home. Carol was the Romper Room hostess for a TV station while we were in Tallahassee. She also had a radio and TV show, "Carol's Coffee Corner", in Tallahassee after the kids were older. She was also the spokesperson for Tradewell Groceries in Seattle for a number of years and did a lot of other commercial work on both radio and TV.

And she has always done a lot of church, civic and volunteer work outside the home. But, when the children were younger, she was always there for them. And she still is.

I could never figure out how both parents could have a career and also raise young children. Many are trying, nowadays. And I suppose some are doing so with success.

Here's what we try to do in our situation. The football season doesn't go on forever. Basically, with preseason practice, the season itself, then recruiting, winter conditioning and spring practice, it's about 10 months — August through May.

In June and July we really work hard at getting quality time as a family and do things together.

Our oldest is son Jeff who is now with Boeing in Seattle. Despite some major physical problems when he was a youngster, Jeff won the state "Pitch, Throw and

Hit" competition when we lived in Colorado and I took him to Dallas for the national finals.

Jeff went to college at Kent State where he met and married his wife Rosemary. They have three children, Jeffrey, Anna and Rebecca.

Rosemary's father, Rudy Malandro, was chairman of the accounting department at Kent State. Rosemary is a CPA and is teaching accounting at Bellevue Community College here in the Seattle area.

Oldest Daughter Jill, who was a field hockey scholarship athlete at Kent State, married another Jeff — my present quarterback coach Jeff Woodruff. They have three children — sons Jared and Jordon and daughter Jessica.

Jill was a state age-group pentathlon winner when she was in junior high school in Colorado. The program wasn't available when we moved to Ohio so she concentrated on field hockey. She also played on the college tennis team.

Jill and her husband Jeff were both just freshmen in college when they married. After high school, Jeff moved out to Seattle and worked in the summer, then went to junior college in Everett and played football there. After junior college they both went back to Kent State. He also played football there until he got injured. He then coached as a student assistant his last year or two.

Youngest daughter Jeni got married this past winter while she was a senior at the University of Washington and a cheerleader for the Huskies. She is now a flight attendant for Alaska Airlines. Her husband, Jim Heckman, owns a sports publishing company.

I spent as much time with Jill as any of the kids because of her pentathlon activity. It was also fun working with Jeff during his little league baseball years. I even gave up golf during that time. I really did find it fun to work out with my own kids.

Daughter Jill as a young
pentathlete and son Jeff
as a Little Leaguer.

Although I wouldn't wish the experiences on anyone, I feel that several family situations that we endured and survived helped draw our family closer together.

When Jeff was six years old we found that he had a bone disease and he had to go into a leg brace for about four years. It was a very traumatic time.

Now, although one leg is slightly shorter than the other and the foot on that leg is a full shoe size smaller, he runs marathons and was in our party that climbed Mt. Rainier.

The medical term for what Jeff had is legge perthes disease. I was coaching at Florida State at the time. We had gone up to play Virginia Tech. While we were away over the weekend, Jeff was staying with our neighbor, a former FSU football player named Mike Norman. They said they had become concerned because Jeff had started to limp. We don't know if he got hit while he was playing football with the other kids, or what happened.

We watched him for a week or 10 days. By that time he was limping even more. He'd throw his foot out as he walked. We took him to a Dr. Holland there in Tallahassee and found out he had legge perthes.

The disease is a deterioration of the ball in the hip joint. The x-rays looked like he had a piece of swiss cheese in there instead of good solid bone.

Remember Chester on TV's Gunsmoke? Remember how he walked? That's what happens if the problem is not corrected. The hip socket will cement itself to the top of the leg bone. From then on they are crippled.

The doctor said it had to be treated immediately. They put him in a complete leg brace for four years. The brace was designed to take all the weight off of his leg and hip joint.

One of the treatments back then was to put the child in traction for two or three years. We just didn't find that as an acceptable alternative for a young kid who was so active.

But the brace never slowed him down. He played baseball. He rode his bike. He did everything the other kids did — and more.

Jeff climbed a tall tree one time. None of the other kids in the neighborhood could shimmy up that tree, but he did. But, because of the brace, he couldn't get down. We thought we were going to have to call the fire department to rescue him. We finally managed without them.

Although the problem never held him back, it was difficult on the family. He wasn't allowed to put any weight on that leg for four years. When he didn't have the brace on he used crutches.

He had a miraculous recovery and played football, basketball and baseball in high school. Jeff was an excellent baseball player in high school. In fact, at one time, when we were in Colorado, he was chosen to the state all-star team that played in a national tournament.

Despite the prolonged leg problems with Jeff, that experience almost paled in comparison when our younger daughter Jeni almost died three years ago at age 19.

In fact, the doctors say she is fortunate to be alive today. She had a lung abscess. She aspirated, of all things, a piece of a cracker. It got lodged in her lung and an infection set in behind it.

One night we were at our beach house and she woke up in the night, bent over in pain. She had just made cheerleader at Washington, which was a dream of hers fulfilled. She thought the pain was from pulling a muscle during the cheerleader tryouts. She was bent over, lying on the floor. That was when the problem first really hit.

At first, the doctors thought she had pneumonia. But it went on and on. Antibiotics had no effect on the problem. It turned out to be a long ordeal. Eventually,

After regaining her health, Jeni followed in Carol's footsteps
when she became a college cheerleader.

we were referred to a pulmonary specialist. Carol took Jeni to see him this one afternoon. He told her to bring Jeni in the next morning for a cat scan.

For about 10 days prior to that, Jeni was having big swings in temperature. She would get a terrible fever. Her temperature would go up to 104 degrees, accompanied by a horrible cough where she would spit up ugly looking phlegm. Then, just as suddenly, her temperature would go back down to near normal. This big fluctuation would happen four or five times a day.

On the way home from the doctor's office her temperature went zooming up again. She told her mom she couldn't get out of the car. Carol called our other daughter, Jill, and told her that "something is happening to Jeni and I'm really scared." Carol asked Jill to stay by her phone in case she was needed.

When Carol went back to the car Jeni said, "Mom, please take me for one last ride around the lake." Now that's a scary statement from a 19-year-old. Almost a premonition of death as we look back on it now. Carol says she couldn't help but have the feeling that both she and Jeni knew she was dying.

Carol tried to keep her spirits up by talking to her while taking her on the drive she requested. When they got home, Jeni managed to get out of the car. Carol helped her to the sofa, but when she got her on the sofa, Jeni became delirious. She was in great pain. Carol put ice water on her, got her back in the car and rushed her to the emergency room. Carol reached me at an alumni golf outing and I raced to the hospital.

The doctor put Jeni in the cat scan and they found this thing — they didn't know what it was — in her lung. He then had Jeni sit on the side of the hospital bed. He took a skewer — a long narrow spike-like thing, like you do shiskabobs on, only longer. It had a rubber hose hooked onto it.

The doctor said, "Now, Jeni, hold real still because I will be working close to your heart. He couldn't put her out. They used only a local anesthetic. Maybe the doctor felt they didn't have time. Then he took this skewer and pierced it through her back and into the lung.

Carol was holding her hands. I have to admit that Jill and I went out into the hall. I couldn't stand to watch.

After he plunged this skewer in, he pulled it out, leaving the rubber hose in her lung. Even out in the hall I was almost overcome by the rancid smell. Puss came out of that hose in such a spurt that it flew all over the walls of the room.

The doctor told us later on that evening that "if you had waited until the appointment tomorrow morning you would have found her dead in her bed. The lung would have ruptured and she would have drowned. This is the sickest I've ever seen anybody be without dying."

For about 10 days in the hospital they had a pump on her, pumping the infection out of that lung.

Jeni later remembered the incident that caused the whole problem. But it was something she didn't give any thought to at the time it occurred. She was eating a cracker when one of her sorority sisters made her laugh. She laughed herself out of breath and quickly inhaled — which we have all done. But she had some chewed up cracker, but not yet swallowed, in her mouth. For about a week she kept coughing. She wasn't really sick, but just kept coughing. But she never related it to the laughing incident.

That whole episode was a very scary thing. The doctor said that if she had been a smoker or not in tip-top condition, she'd have been dead long before the problem was diagnosed.

Certainly one of the most difficult times for me, maybe even more difficult than dealing with Jeni's brush with death, is something I have never before

At daughter Jeni's wedding on Dec. 9, 1990.

From the left: Son Jeff and his wife Rosemary with children Jeffrey and Anna Marie. (Missing is youngest grandchild Rebecca James.) After me, Carol and the bride is newest son-in-law Jim Heckman; then daughter Jill, her husband Jeff Woodruff and their three children, Jordan, Jessica and Jared.

shared publicly. I do so now in the hope that it can help and comfort others.

When I was coaching at Kent State, my father committed suicide.

It happened toward the end of my first season. Things weren't going too well. We had only won three games. We were getting ready to go on the road to play Toledo.

After Thursday's practice I hurried home to change clothes. I was to give a talk at a dinner for a group of boosters.

The phone rang. It was my brother Art. He told me dad had shot himself. It was, naturally, a traumatic shock. I told Carol to get ready to leave, that I would be back in about 30 or 40 minutes. I had to draw on all of my inner strength. Getting to Massillon as fast as I could — or an hour later — wasn't going to help matters. My brothers were already there.

So I went to the dinner and told the person in charge that I had a family crisis and asked if I could make my remarks right away rather than after the meal. Although I didn't tell them what the crisis was, they of course said that would be fine and I quickly delivered what had to be the most difficult speech of my life, then excused myself and left.

The newspapers respected our request and feelings and kept the news of his death off the sports pages. The obituary said it was due to a self-inflicted gun shot wound. Those who read that knew what had happened, but since Massillon was 40 miles from Kent, it wasn't very commonly known.

My brothers and I have never before chosen to "go public" with the fact that his death was a suicide. But I have come to the conclusion that sometimes you can help people suffering under similar circumstances by letting them know that others have had to deal with the same situation.

Carol and I have tried to help others who have suffered through the same tragedy in their family. When we tell them about my father they say, "We never dreamed you folks had ever faced adversity like that in your lives." If my talking about it here helps just one family, it will have been worthwhile.

Each person in his own way, when this happens, tends to blame themselves. Of course they shouldn't do so because it isn't the "fault" of anyone, but even I thought at the time that my having taken the Kent State job, and then having a bad season, had depressed my father and caused him to do this.

After I came to Seattle, my mother also passed away the day before a football game. It was the Friday before we met UCLA in 1975.

Mom suffered a heart attack and a stroke while I was flying to Seattle for my interview before being named the Washington coach. That was another trying time. As I related earlier, we had a difficult airplane trip and were hours late in arriving in Seattle.

Like the situation with my father, there wasn't anything I could do about mother's situation except do the best I could in Seattle and then return home.

She came out of that attack pretty well, but died the next fall.

It seems sometimes as though I was being put to a special test. My father died during my first season as the head coach at Kent State and my mother died during my first season at Washington.

We also had a coach's wife die in childbirth while we were at Kent State. That was also a very trying time for everybody. I happened to be the only one they could find who had the exact same blood type as she. The doctors felt a transfusion, rather than just plasma, might help. I was glad to be a donor. Unfortunately, it didn't save her.

I also had a little health problem three years ago or so, but I'm really in fine shape now. Dick Scesniak,

Despite some heartaches and tragedy, our children — and now their children —
bring much joy to our lives.
Here are the grandparents with (from left): Jordan, Jessica, Anna, Jeffrey and Jared.

who was with us for years, was the head coach at Kent State when he died of a heart attack very suddenly. Dave McClain, who was the head coach at Wisconsin, died about three weeks later.

One of our boosters, Dave Cohn who is presently on the board of regents, suggested I should have a stress test. He had a heart attack himself not long before that but was getting along fine.

I decided I had probably reached the age where I should at least begin getting an annual physical. Everything checked out fine. Dr. John Mazzarella, my cardiologist, told me to come back in a couple of years. Which I did in 1989.

This time, when going through the treadmill test, the doctor discovered an arrhythmia problem. My heart rate elevated rapidly when I exercised. I took a beta blocker for a period of time and that totally resolved the problem. I'm not on any medication now.

All of us have hard times and stressful situations during our lifetime. I think it's how you come out of them that is important. And, I'm happy to report, the James family is getting along very well.

chapter twenty

Introducing the President proved
conclusively to me that
football and politics don't mix

After sharing a platform with Ronald Reagan and George Bush when they were president and vice-president of the United States, I learned that football and politics don't mix.

I didn't think I was getting that involved in politics when I did what I did. I thought I was only honoring the offices they held — not promoting the men who happened to hold those offices.

But plenty of other people, and surprisingly some in the academic community at the university, obviously thought otherwise.

The whole thing started right after it was announced that Vice-President Bush was going to make an appearance in Seattle.

I got a call from the White House and they asked me if I would consider introducing him at a meeting. A former Kent State student was working as an aide and gave the campaign committee the idea. It's true that he

Carol and me with then Vice-President George Bush

and Reagan were running for re-election. But this was
to be an open forum meeting. My only job was to introduce him. I wasn't going to make any kind of political
speech. I was just going to introduce the vice-president
of the United States. I thought that would be great. So
I accepted.

I had a chance to visit and be with him before the
event. I got a set of vice presidential cuff links which I
have among our mementos in our home. Then we had
our picture taken together.

I came out and gave a brief introduction of his
achievements and offices held. He came out. I gave
him the microphone, sat down and enjoyed the evening.
That was it.

The event was primarily a question and answer af-
fair. I was very impressed by the way he handled himself. The questions ranged on a wide variety of subjects.
There were questions on everything. He has such a tremendous background. Even so, I was amazed at how informed he was on so many different subjects.

When it was over, Carol and I were in the back
room with all the security people. We had left our car
downtown. Somebody had driven us over there. Next
thing we knew, the vice-president was inviting us to
ride back downtown with him in his limousine. We
thought that would be great.

We got in the back seat with him, just the three of
us. People were all lined up to see the vice-president. It
was fun to see how he could communicate with the people outside. Through a two-way speaker system, he
could hear what they were saying and he could chat
back to them. The windows were thick and obviously
bullet proof.

We had a very nice, down-to-earth talk with him on
the way back downtown. We talked about a lot of
things. He had been the speaker at the Heisman Trophy banquet in New York a few weeks earlier. I remember we talked about that. I also remember Carol

asking if he planned on running for President in four years. He said he and Barbara would be considering it strongly.

A couple of days later I got a nice note from him. On the stationery it said, "Vice President of the United States. Aboard Air Force II. 10-19-84".

The note said: "Dear Don: Thanks ever so much for introducing me at the forum. I really appreciated that. And I loved our visit in the car. Best of luck to you in the weeks ahead. Gratefully, George Bush."

A week or two later, President Reagan was coming out to Seattle for a speaking engagement. The White House called again. Apparently they felt the Bush visit had gone okay, so I said yes, I would also introduce the president.

About that time I got to thinking about it, wondering whether I should get involved with a re-election campaign for the President. The White House called back. They said the situation had changed. "We've got a problem," the spokesman said, "because the Governor of the State of Washington is a Republican." Instead of asking the football coach to introduce the president, they obviously felt they should ask the Governor.

They wanted to know if I would make some sort of a presentation instead. Possibly give him an autographed football and a Husky hat. I said I'd like to think about it and then get back to them.

I wanted to do it. After all it was the president of the United States. I wanted to meet him and have my family have the chance to meet him. I didn't think it was as though I was making a campaign speech myself. I didn't think of him as a candidate, but rather as the president! And I was being given the opportunity to meet him and hear him talk.

I talked to some people who were close to our program — some boosters who I have a lot of respect for. I asked them if they thought I should do it or if it would be unwise to get involved.

I was heavily criticized for giving an autographed football to President Ronald Reagan. Governor John Spellman looked on.

They all said they thought the people would respect the fact that I was getting the honor of being with the president of the United States. That it was the office, not the man. They didn't think it would be an issue. So I did it.

And a couple of weeks later I received a nice note that said: "I was delighted to be in Seattle recently and the warm welcome I received made me feel right at home. Many thanks for the autographed football which you presented to me at the Seattle Center. What a terrific remembrance from my friends at the University of Washington. Please convey my appreciation to your team for the thoughtful gesture. Best heartfelt wishes to everyone. Ronald Reagan"

I also got a lot of other mail. And the phone about rang off the hook. People really came down on me over the incident. Really bad. Not just a few. A lot of people were upset. Democrats and people that no doubt were opposed to President Reagan and his program.

I had many people who backed me, of course, and others who were against what I had done. It was a big mess and here we were getting ready to play a football game. This was during the fall. It was very difficult to deal with. I felt like the people who called deserved an explanation and an answer.

A number of faculty called, critical of what I had done. I thought they were wrong and still do. I don't know how a faculty member could ever criticize me after the things that I have witnessed on college campuses during the past 32 years. I really felt a need to tell them how I felt. I didn't want to take the time to write a lot of letters. So I was taking phone calls and again, right in the middle of game preparation. I probably shouldn't have done that.

It was also extremely stressful on Cleo Blackstone, my secretary at the time. She had the normal work of getting practice and game plans out in addition to the calls and mail on the political issue.

It didn't change anything, but it made me feel better when I received the following personal note among all the hate mail:

"Dear Don: I was sorry to read that you have come under fire for introducing me and President Reagan at our recent visits. I wish there was a way I could rally to your defense. It was great being with you and your wife and I will never forget your coming all the way over to West Seattle to give me that introduction. Warm regards, George Bush."

Among the other mail, however, was a letter from a guy who said that I was rich and that I didn't know what it was like to be poor and suffer financially.

I couldn't wait to write him back and explain my childhood and how I lived in a garage for eight years with no indoor plumbing. And to let him know that I did know what poor was. I added that if I have any affluency now, it's because of the great country we live in and the opportunity that we are afforded.

It was mind boggling to me that people could be mad at me because I got to meet the president of the United States. I didn't say anything. I didn't get a chance to say anything. I just congratulated him and gave him the autographed ball.

I had one lawyer write a scathing letter saying I should be fined by the state for giving away state property. He said he was a University of Washington graduate and that he was a contributor to the university. But, he added, he wasn't going to continue to contribute if these kinds of things were happening.

I looked up his name in the gift giving records. As I recall, he had given a grand total of $28 to the University of Washington. Incidentally, I paid for the football and hat so that no state monies were involved.

Another thing that happened is that when upper campus became critical of what I did, then a large

Carol thought we were No. 1 after beating Oklahoma in the Orange Bowl
to conclude the 1984 season. So did a lot of other people.

number of football fans — who were no doubt Republicans — began writing letters getting after our administration for getting on me.

Anyway, those are the kind of things that I had to deal with. It was traumatic.

Fortunately, things went better on the football field. That was 1984 when we went 11-1, beat Oklahoma in the Orange Bowl and wound up ranked No. 2 in the nation behind BYU.

A lot of people felt we should have been rated ahead of BYU for having played a tougher schedule. But, BYU won 12 games and we won 11. Besides, I have no control over the decision the voters make. If Bo — and Michigan — had just beaten BYU in the Holiday Bowl, we'd have been a lock for No. 1.

But, there are always a lot of "ifs", "should haves" and "could haves" in sports as there are in life.

chapter twenty one

*I got "roped in" to
climbing Mt. Rainier
and running a marathon*

Golf has always been my favorite personal participation sport. After climbing a mountain and running a marathon, golf is even more solidly No. 1 with me.

I have always tried to work hard at staying fit. Jogging has been an integral part of that conditioning. When I worked up to running Seattle's annual Emerald City marathon in 1987 — at the urging of my son Jeff — I managed that feat with very little public notice.

Not so when it came to climbing Mt. Rainier. That event almost became a media spectacle.

Dr. Steve Bramwell, our team physician, had tried to climb the mountain the year before but ran into bad weather and didn't get to make it all the way to the top.

Later, he and I were talking about it. I don't know what got into me but I said, "Geez, I'd like to try that." I guess I always thought it would be a fun thing to try. He explained that he was acting as the doctor and advisor for a group of Seattle area climbers who were training to climb Mt. Everest the next year.

Steve thought he might be able to get them to guide the football coaches up Mt. Rainier, if some of the other guys wanted to join me. He thought that we might be able to get the Mt. Everest hopefuls some publicity since they needed to raise nearly $500,000 to finance their Mt. Everest expedition.

Doc talked to the climbers and I talked to the coaches. The climbers were agreeable and Rich Huegli, Bob Stull, Trent Walters, Gary Pinkel and Jeff Woodruff from the coaching staff, plus my accountant Jack Hammack, agreed to make the climb.

By the time we were ready to start our training, we had 48 people ready to climb the mountain. And 17 of them were from the media! Mt. Rainier is 14,000 feet above sea level, so it required that we spend two nights on the mountain before making our final trip to the summit. Yet we had people up there doing live TV shows.

The preparation was fun. First we attended some instructional classes in mountaineering techniques, including the use of crampons, ice axes and climbing ropes. Then, a month or two before the actual climb, they took us up to the mountain where we learned what they call "arresting" techniques.

Basically, you have to learn how to stop a fall. You have this pick you carry. If you slip and fall, you have to learn to get over on your stomach and dig in. They found a real steep runoff that went down 30 or 40 yards and then flattened out. There was no way we would really get hurt in that situation because we'd stop after sliding down a ways. The idea is to learn how to stop yourself before you get to the bottom.

During the practice session, they would put us in a lot of different body positions. You have to learn to get on your stomach with your feet down the mountain. Then the trick is to dig in with your pick to stop your fall.

Climbing Mt. Rainier once was enough

First, they'd just have us lie on our stomach, start sliding and then stop ourselves. Then they had us start sliding down on our back. You have to learn how to turn over before digging in with the pick. They also had us do some somersaults and then go down backwards.

They taught us how to get stopped and out of trouble in case we really fell during the climb. There was also a lot of fitness training. That summer Carol and I bought a van in Frankfurt, Germany. During that trip, the two Jeffs — my son and son-in-law — and I did a lot of training.

We'd get up in the morning and run. Son Jeff would always load up his pack with clothes, cameras and other needs for the day. I didn't do enough of that. Because during the actual climb, when you add the weight of a 50-pound pack on your back, and you climb with all that gear, it becomes a lot tougher. Especially when you get above 10,000 feet and the air is thinner.

The crazy thing is that after all that training and preparation, I almost didn't make the climb which was set to start the last weekend of July in 1983. Jim Lambright and I were at a clinic in Tuscaloosa, Alabama, earlier that week. After it was over, they flew us in a private plane over to Memphis to get our flight back. In Memphis, without any notice or explanation, the airline took our crew off of our plane and cancelled the flight.

I was really depressed. I'd spent all this time in fitness training to climb Mt. Rainier and then the night before we were supposed to go I couldn't get home.

I was standing in line next to some guy who listened to my complaints. He said there had to be a way to get us back to Seattle. He got the reservation agent to check out an idea and we found we could go through LA and then go standby on the last flight out of LA for Seattle.

And that's what we did. I think we got back to Seattle at 4 a.m., then had to be at a breakfast for the climbers at seven back at Southcenter before we took off.

I barely had time to go home, get my gear and take off again. In my hurry I was stopped for speeding on the way home. But, after the policeman heard my story, he let me continue after asking that I observe a more reasonable speed. He had me clocked at over 85 miles an hour.

So, I was up all night flying home and then started out to climb Mt. Rainier.

But it worked out. All 48 of us made it to the top. That was a great accomplishment in itself. We were told that just over half — 54 percent to be exact — of the people who attempt the climb make it to the top. They say that technically it's not a difficult mountain to conquer, but the thin air gets to you. It takes a lot of endurance to make it to the 14,410-foot elevation level.

It was a special feat for those guys carrying the TV equipment. Although I think the stations hired some experienced climbers to take the gear up the mountain.

We climbed in group of three. Each group had to have a tent and cooking utensils, plus the ropes and all of the gear that each climber needed for his personal safety. We lived on the mountain two nights, so that meant food to carry as well. My guide was Warren Thompson and our other tent partner was Jack Hammack.

It was quite an experience. There were no serious accidents. No group fell. The snow bridges over the crevasses all held, so nobody crashed in. The guides had some worry about that the second day, however. They got us up at one o'clock in the morning to start climbing. That was so the snow bridges would be firm and not melted by the daytime sun. We all had lights on our hats. The early start was necessary because we had to get to the summit and back down across the Ingraham Glacier — that's where the large crevasses are —

before the sun started to soften and melt the snow bridges.

Two years before our climb, in that area of the Ingraham Glacier, 11 climbers were killed when an avalanche of ice broke loose and buried them in a crevasse. Since record-keeping began in 1899, the mountain has claimed nearly 300 lives.

I have to admit that when you go over the snow bridges it isn't a whole lot of fun. You're roped together. The No. 1 guy goes across. If the bridge fell in, the other two could save him. Then if No. 2 falls, No. 1 and No. 3 are on each side of the crevasse so they can pull him up. With two guys across, then No. 3 can go.

They had also taught us the technique of how to climb out of one of those crevasses in case we fell.

Bob Stull, who is now the head coach at Missouri, stumbled at a rather critical spot, but his guide and coach Gary Pinkel, his other rope partner, dug in and prevented any real problem from occurring.

As I said earlier, I had been a jogger for several years. It was an important part of my fitness training. In fact, my son Jeff started jogging and trained and ran in a couple of marathons.

There are a lot of ways to train for a marathon. Jeff was taking his long runs on the weekends. He'd follow his normal jogging routine during the week, then maybe run eight miles on Saturday or Sunday. The next week he'd extend it to nine. The idea is to keep extending each week until you get up to about the marathon distance.

Well, I started the same regimen. I got up to 17 miles. That's the most I'd ever run — by far. And I was in pretty good shape. I was doing a lot of running during the week and getting along okay. I was logging a lot of miles. And, after my long run on the weekend, it didn't take long to recover. I felt pretty good. When I'd get back home I was tired, but I could rest for awhile and then bounce back pretty quickly.

But the marathon that spring was just a couple of weeks away. That's the time when you are supposed to taper back. I realized that if I had another month to train I could probably make it. So I set that as a goal for the next year.

So, in the winter of 1987 I started the training a little earlier. That meant I had to do it during recruiting season which is December, January and February. No matter where I was, I'd get my run in — sometimes early in the morning, sometimes late at night.

I was nervous about 26 miles. But my longest training run, two weeks before the marathon, was 22 miles. And, despite being 54 years old at the time, I made that without difficulty. In fact, during my two heavy weeks just before that, I ran 70 and 72 miles. Those were my two big buildup, peak weeks. And I probably didn't have to run quite that much.

Then I tapered off. And I felt good and rested when the race began. My goal was to finish, upright. And to finish under four hours, which I did. I think I just wanted to prove to myself that I could do it.

So, at the age of 54, I ran my first — and probably my last marathon.

The media didn't make a big deal out of that like they did the mountain climb. Which was okay with me. I tried to keep it low key. I think the media went along on the Mt. Rainier climb so they would be on hand to cover the event in case I or one of my coaches went sailing down the mountain. The climbers had a joke that when you fell there is the 100-foot rule. If you don't get stopped within 100 feet, you probably won't get stopped.

chapter twenty two

*My favorite sport
away from football
is golf — and more golf*

Although I only get to play golf a few months of the year, I really enjoy the game. It's my favorite pastime.

Normally, the clubs don't come out of the closet until after spring practice and I put them back on the shelf by the end of July. Some coaches play golf outings in August before practice starts. For me, that's football time.

I've been down to a seven handicap the last three or four years. I've had a couple of real good rounds on decent courses. I've had two 71s and a couple of 72s during the last few years. You always hope you can go out and duplicate that. That's the fun. I feel real good about my game and enjoy golf whenever I can break 80.

The tough part is playing for three months and then putting the clubs away.

We have quite a few golf outings around the state with our booster groups in late May and the early part of the summer. And I'll do a few men's days at various

Golf: My favorite sport away from football

clubs. Those events are coordinated by the Alumni Office.

My assistant coach who recruits that particular area of the state will accompany me. Also, many times alumni director Jon Rider, Pete Liske from the Tyee Club, and basketball coach Lynn Nance will go along.

I enjoy golf so much it doesn't bother me to play golf with three alums who want to talk football — as long as they don't talk on my back swing.

The thing that does bother me is that I then have to go listen to myself speak at the dinner after golf. Every night, night after night, it's the same thing, reviewing the personnel and the upcoming season.

Lynn Nance and I get to the point where we laugh sometimes. We've heard each other so much that I have said, "Tonight you give my spiel and I'll give yours." One night, Lynn got on first and used my lines and my jokes. He got a lot of laughs out of them. Then I got up and was stuck.

But we have a lot of fun out of it. And meet a lot of wonderful people.

It's especially fun after a year like this last one, with a good season and a Rose Bowl victory. The response and attendance is great and everything is a lot more upbeat.

Later in the summers, on our family vacations, I've had the opportunity to play some of the finest courses in the world. I've played in Scotland at St. Andrews, Troon, Turnberry and Preswick. I had the chance to play both Port Monarch and the Dublin Country Club in Ireland and I played in France down at the Cannes Country Club and at Sotogrande on the coast of Spain.

At the other end of the world I have played in Bangkok, in Seoul, Korea, and also at a course just outside Hong Kong.

I would guess that one of the big thrills was playing Pine Valley, which is located near Philadelphia, but is actually in New Jersey. That course, in the opinion of

With radio-TV personality Dennis James (no relation) at a Bogey Buster golf tournament

most experts, is ranked the No. 1 course in the world. And I've had the chance to play it three times.

In California, I've played Pebble Beach and the Olympic Club in San Francisco. I haven't golfed at Cypress Point, but I did play Spyglass down there. Also, LaCosta in San Diego.

I love the golf courses in the Orlando area. Played Lake Nona and Grand Cypress. Also, Bay Hill — where I met Arnold Palmer — and I've played on his new course at Isleworth. In 1991, I also got to play in the Seniors Pro-Am in Palm Springs at the Vintage Course.

Another favorite among the more famous courses in the country is the Firestone course in Ohio.

I was playing a round on the coast of Spain at a country club in Marbalia one summer and ran into Sean Connery.

I haven't had the opportunity to play with a lot of pros or celebrities. Oh, I've played in pro-ams and that kind of thing. I've met Julie Inkster and visited with her at a Coach of the Year event the year I was president of the American Football Coaches Association. I have also played golf with Don Bies, a local golf professional.

A real favorite is a tournament in Ohio called the "Bogey Buster". There I played with astronaut Gene Cernan and Dennis James, among others.

At that event you'd get on the bus to go out to the course and there'd be Jose Ferrar, Perry Como, Charlie Pride, Glen Campbell and a lot of other celebrities. I didn't play with all that many, but I was around them a lot for three or four days for several years in a row.

As I said, my problem is that about the time I get my game in pretty good shape it's time for football. But I do enjoy the game and the chance I've had to play on so many great courses.

I suppose my main claim to fame is having had three holes-in-one.

The first came at the Elms Country Club in Massillon. It was a fairly short hole, about 135 yards as I remember. I was in my 20s and just getting started in golf at the time.

In 1979 I had one at the Fairwood Country Club here in the Seattle area. It was during a tournament and they were offering an Oldsmobile Cutlass for a hole-in-one.

Not only was the hole over 200 yards, but you couldn't even see the bottom of the flagstick from the tee. Obviously assuming that nobody would have a chance of getting a hole-in-one on such a hole, the dealer giving the car away didn't take out insurance against it happening.

After I hit a good five-wood, I got pretty excited. Our whole group could see it was going to be close. As we approached the green we couldn't see the ball and then everybody got excited. I didn't think it was long enough because the hole was so long. But, sure enough, we found it in the cup.

For a year I became a non-amateur for winning that big a prize, but then I applied with the United States Golf Association for reinstatement as an amateur.

Later I got my third hole-on-one at the Ranier Country Club here in the Seattle area. That was a much shorter hole. As a remember I hit a 9-iron or a wedge.

Having played so many different courses, people often asked which is my favorite.

Although several are probably "better" courses, when you walk onto the first tee at St. Andrews you get a feeling that can't be matched elsewhere. That is where it all started!

But we've got a lot of great courses right here in the Northwest that don't have to take a back seat to any of them.

We've got the water, the mountains, the streams and lakes. And many great picturesque golf courses have been developed right here at home.

chapter twenty three

*My coaching philosophy
has developed over
the length of my career*

The development of the coaching philosophy and style that I have today started way back when I was a high school player. The No. 1 thing I learned at Massillon was to work at football the year around. It's not a three-month game. Chuck Mather, my high school coach, had a reputation of being highly organized. If you asked people close to our program, that would probably be one of the first things they'd say about me.

Mather was a real detail guy. And it was such a highly organized high school program at Massillon. We didn't just run a few plays. We had a big thick play book. And we had structured game plans and scouting reports.

You would normally have to be in coaching for a fairly long period of time before you become real philosophical about the way you were going to run the ball, throw the ball or play defense. But I learned a lot about the game even at the high school level.

Unlike a lot of coaches, I only have our players practice in pads on Tuesdays and Wednesdays during the season. We're in sweats on Monday and Thursday and we don't practice at all on Fridays when we're at home. That's a real departure from most programs.

When we travel, we have a 30-minute practice on Friday after our arrival. It's really used as an opportunity to get our players accustomed to the field and to loosen up from the trip. We have three different kinds of artificial surfaces in our league and five fields have grass. We don't get on grass a whole lot. And, late in the season, we may not get out to practice on grass because of weather. So the Friday workout gives us a chance to get the grass shoes on and cut a little bit.

The absence of a Friday practice at home comes from my feeling that the rest is more important than any benefit the players might get from a workout. It's another demand on their time and if you're not going to accomplish something from the workout, then why do anything.

If we were going to have a Friday workout, even just to limber up, the players would still have to go through the ankle taping process, get dressed, practice, shower and dress again. It's really a mental lift for them not to have to do that. I picked up that idea while serving as an assistant to Eddie Crowder at Colorado.

We do meet that afternoon. In fact, the players take a written test about the game plan for Saturday's opponent. We give them a final scouting report and I do a final substitution review.

My main talk to the team, however, is on Thursday. That's when I get into the psychology of the game. I break the Thursday talk down in general announcements first, things they've got to hear about, mention that dress lists will be posted along with who will be going to the hotel for Friday night before home games.

The second thing I do is give them an update on the conference stats. Which team is leading each category and where we stand and where Saturday's opponent stands. I touch on kickoff and punt returns, penalties, fourth quarter — the points we score late in the games and the same for our opponent. I do that to stress the importance of proper conditioning. I give them a quick comparison. I comment on where we need to improve.

Then I break down the opponent and how I personally feel about their offense, defense, kicking, and their coaching staff.

Then I try to pick up on a theme. I've used a ton of them over the years. Just as an example, one year I saw the workout schedule of Dan Gabel, the gold medal wrestler who became the coach at Iowa. He had great self motivation. So I talked about his work ethics, something the players would do well to model themselves after.

I talk about a lot of things that deal with effort and intensity, courage, the concentration of competition and things like that. I've told about great athletes and great victories. Anything that I can wind into a story that may get their attention and give some of the players a lift.

I try to vary the major points each week, and even from season to season, so the players wouldn't say, "Here he goes again with the same old stuff." I've kept the outline from every Thursday talk for nearly 20 years. Every single one. That way I can look back and make sure I am giving them new ideas for the mental and physical preparation for the upcoming game.

I learned from Bill Peterson at Florida State that to try to psych up the players with a fiery speech just before the game on Saturday is too late. He was convinced that if a coach even waited until Friday for such a talk, it was too late. The players don't have enough time in 24 hours to mentally react to what you're saying.

The later you put your game face on the less effect it will have. I've been around players who put on their game face by Wednesday or even Tuesday. To me, the time you put it on means the time you can't think of anything else but the game.

Some people might wait until game day, or right before the kickoff. But the great ones, the consistent competitors, they kick back into Thursday. We want them to go to class and do their homework, but I tell them, "From now until game time, you don't need to be entertained, you don't need to go to parties. Now's the time to take the film and master your plan and master your opponent."

To me, a pre-game pep talk is really too late. When the whistle blows and the ball is kicked off you had better be prepared or you will not perform well.

On game day I try to pick up on something that was covered on Thursday. The players don't have to listen to a speech. It's just one or two points prior to going on the field for the kickoff.

Taking the team to a Friday movie is a long-standing tradition with most programs. I grew up on that myself. The theory has been to get their minds off of football. But I think times have changed and we need to keep the player's mind on football.

Besides, the movies are generally so bad. My last Friday night movie was at Northern Illinois when I was coaching at Kent State. It was the worst movie I could ever imagine. It was full of sex and brutal murders. And we played awful the next day. I don't know if it was the movie or not, but it was not healthy or the kind of thing young people need to see. So I said, "That's it," and I haven't taken the players to a Friday night movie since.

Instead, we turn our attention back to football. We go to Bellevue and stay at the Greenwood Inn for home games. We stayed there for a long time, then changed and went across the street to another hotel for about three years. But a couple of times they booked in some convention and wanted to move us to another location.

I admit to being structured. I didn't like having our routine changed, so we went back to the Greenwood Inn.

It's not a superstitious thing. But I have to admit that I remember how I do certain things. If we had a good week and won, I'm going to continue to jog the same route I did the week before and pretty much stay on the same schedule. If we had a bad week, I'm likely to change things. I don't know if that's superstition or just a routine. But as long as the routine is producing good results, I stick with it.

The total organization of our program is probably patterned more after Bill Peterson at Florida State than any other single coach, and that means it goes back to Paul Dietzel. Bill worked with him at LSU when they had a national championship team in 1958 with Billy Cannon, who won the Heisman Trophy that season. I also learned a lot about defensive football from Perry Moss when I first went to Florida State.

Then, as I moved on to Michigan, I got a taste of the Fritz Crisler-Bump Elliott era and how they did things and their philosophy. I think maybe Bump is the most compassionate coach I've been around. He seemed to really have the player's best interest at heart. He's the kind of man you'd want to play for — or have your son play for.

After that I worked with Eddie Crowder at Colorado. He had an Oklahoma background through Bud Wilkinson, although the system Eddie had established at Colorado was a little different. So it was helpful for me to see how that worked.

I thought Eddie had an ability to determine which part of the overall scheme was not functioning right and work on that part. The whole thing, of course, must be properly tuned. There may be one or two parts that are causing the unit to break down — whether it's offense, defense, or kicking.

Eddie also taught me not to be unrealistic. If you have a player out there who is giving everything he has, but he just isn't capable of being a great player, don't ask or expect him to give more than he can. Judge him on his ability and his effort to just be as good as he can.

So, as I went along, I tried to pick up on the strong points of each coach I worked with.

Wilkinson's so-called Oklahoma system, which I picked up through Eddie Crowder, called for a little more simplicity in the overall scheme. It is extremely sound and based on the idea of "never beat yourself."

The system impresses on a coach not to cross over the line of what you can get taught and what the players can absorb and learn to do well. Don't go into a game with too much — too many passes, too many runs, or too many coverages.

It says, "We're going to limit what we're going to do, but we're going to do what we do right and not beat ourselves." Another philosophy I have, which differs from many coaches, is that I don't have a single special teams coach. Instead, I take all the assistants who are not coordinators and give each one of them a part of the kicking game. I make each one the head coach of one phase. I have six coaches who are assigned to the six basic special teams — place kicking, defense against place kicking; punting and defense against punting; kickoff and defense against kickoffs. So, all the coaches, including myself, work with the kicking game.

Each "head coach" of a phase of the kicking game can pick any player for his team — unless it's somebody I say he can't have. If he wanted the quarterback, I wouldn't let him go on a special team unless he was a kicker, for instance. They probably couldn't have my No. 1 tailback. But they can basically pick anybody they want for their special teams.

One of the biggest problems is to see that we have enough time to practice those six areas. It's important because the kicking game can influence the outcome of a game as much as offense or defense.

In fact, in most seasons you can only hope to out perform the opponent on offense four, five, maybe six times. You can also hope to do a better job on defense than the opponent in no more than five or six games — unless you have a particularly good unit as we did on defense in '84 and '90.

But, since other coaches may not pay as much attention to special teams, with some attention to detail and devoting a lot of practice time to it, you can expect to do a better job on the kicking game in nine of your 11 games.

During the preparation of our game plan we look for things in the opponent's kicking game. When we are in punt formation, if there is a gap or a hole left open that we can run in, or a flaw we see in the coverage, we'll have a play ready. It doesn't always get called. But we will have a series of trick plays — reverses, a reverse pass, things like that — ready for each game in case they are needed.

There is a difference in philosophy among coaches on punt and kickoff returns. You can have walls. The old punt returns were pretty much wall returns. All the players set a 'picket fence' down one side. Then the return man would try to get between the wall and the sideline.

The biggest change on punt returns has become the man-to-man return. Players are assigned to a man. I'm just going to get on you and hold you up and if we're going to return right, I'm going to block you left. You're my guy. There's no question, all the way. It becomes more of a screen situation. There are also some subtle little traps and crosses people will use.

You've seen teams getting ready to kick off when suddenly one of their players loops around behind the kicker and comes down with the guys on the other side of the ball.

Well, when a team is about to receive a kickoff, everybody counts from one end of the line of players on the kickoff team. Maybe you've got the fourth guy in from the left. But he's the one who, at the last second, loops clear around to the other side of the field. He's trying to foul up your counting system. Do you keep him and follow him clear over to the other side of the field, or do you now take the "new" fourth man from the left? To counteract that, your team has to make a decision as to whether you're going to keep the same guy, no matter where he goes, or are you going to pass him off and zone block.

From watching film of the opponent's previous games, you pretty much know what to expect and thus prepare for it. Most people who use a "looper" on their kickoff team, that's their scheme, and they usually stay with it.

I believe that a lot I say to the players is important and I try to be as prepared as possible. I attempt to say things that will help them become better competitors and better people. I also believe that motivation of all people in our program is the most important thing I do.

I put things in writing that I'm going to say before the game. And things in writing I'm going to say after the game, win or lose. I learned that from Bear Bryant. A long time ago he said that a coach should be prepared to face his team and the media after a game. And you should think ahead of time about what you want to say.

I think some coaches make a mistake by not having thought about what they might say ahead of time. There is so much anger involved after a loss that they may wind up verbally beating up on the players, opponents and officials.

We may have been a three-touchdown underdog and got beat by two points. Even though you lost, you need to look to the positive. After all, the players, in that situation, know they had to have played pretty good. If I would then be highly critical of them I would be making a grave error in the dynamics of developing a team.

Coach Bryant's basic comment was, "You take the blame if you lose and give the credit if you win." That's a pretty good theme to follow regardless of what business you are in. I even put that down on my game card each week.

When I was an assistant at Michigan, Benny Oosterbaan was there. He was retired, but I had the chance to spend quite a bit of time with him. Benny had a great creed about life and football which I have tried to instill in my teams. He always reminded me, "Isn't it wonderful what can be accomplished when no one cares who gets the credit."

I've picked up some others along the way. One of my favorites is, "Life is like a coin. You get to spend it any where and any way you want. But you only get to spend it once." Another is, "The life you live will be the only Bible some people will read." And, "Is what I am doing getting us closer to our objective of winning?" I had that on my desk for many years.

Benny also gave me Fielding Yost's book to read. It was written in 1905. After a long search, I finally found my own copy in an antique book store in San Francisco. That book didn't tell how to defend the pass. But it's amazing how little the basic fundamentals of football and life have changed over of the years.

chapter twenty four

*Every coach has a hand
in preparing our game plan
for the upcoming opponent*

After studying the strengths and weaknesses of an opponent, a well-devised game plan can go a long way toward assuring victory. I have always felt strongly that the preparation of the game plan each week should be a team effort by all the coaches.

Even though, as an assistant, I was always a defensive coordinator, I don't tell my coordinator what I want done. Nor do I just want him to submit a plan to me for my approval.

One of the things I disliked when I was the defensive coordinator, were the number of assistants who relied on other coaches to devise the game plan.

The head coach certainly shouldn't be coming up with all the ideas. Or the coordinator. With nine or ten coaches on the staff and just two idea guys, that means eight others are sleeping through the session.

So, the first thing I established when I was at Kent State, and we still follow this procedure, is make every coach submit a plan. If you are the linebacker coach or

The game plan in this case will be to circle the wagons.
Our coaching staff a few years back picked up on the 'James Gang' theme.

From the left: Trent Walters, now an assistant at Texas A&M; Ray Dorr, the quarterback coach at USC; Skip Hall, head coach at Boise State; John Pease, assistant coach with the New Orleans Saints; the only James boy in the gang; Jim Lambright, UW defensive coordinator; Al Roberts (kneeling), New York Jets assistant; Bob Stull, head coach at Missouri; and Gary Pinkel, head coach at Toledo.

the defensive line coach, I want you to submit a defensive plan for the next game. I want you to look at the same stuff the defensive coordinator and I are looking at. I want you to look at the scouting report and I want you to think. I want you to come up with a plan that will help us win this game. I don't want you to sit in a meeting and do nothing. I want some run defenses, some coverage defenses, some blitzes.

And I ask all of the offensive coaches do the same thing in devising the offensive game plan.

I never have wanted it to be a Don James plan. Even though I am proud of the strengths my coordinators have, they also welcome and need the ideas of the others.

The most critical time of the game planning is Monday night. I usually spend that time with the defensive coaches. If I have some specific ideas or if the offense had trouble in the most recent game, I'll sit in on their meeting as well.

But, if we've been moving the ball, then I let them run with it. I get their game plan, review it, and study it. Obviously, I can make adjustments and changes. I'll usually have a suggestion that they drop a certain play out of the package because it won't work against the defense I expect from the next opponent, or because they are planning to use a play that wouldn't give their defense a problem.

Those Monday night meetings are preceded by a brainstorm session that morning. That's the time when our offensive coaches tell our defensive guys what they see that the next opponent is likely to do that will be tough for them to stop. What they saw in the last game or have seen on film. We're all involved in that. Giving suggestions and ideas to the coaches on the other side of the ball.

As an example, say we just played Cal. Our offense had to contend with Cal's defense. The film of that game is graded on Sunday. We see the adjustments they made.

Now we're going to play UCLA the next week. So we spend the rest of Sunday looking at UCLA.

Now comes the Monday morning brainstorm session. The coaches tell each other what ideas Cal came up with that were tough for us to solve. You can be sure UCLA will be planning to do the same things if were tough for us to solve. And they share things they've discovered that UCLA has been doing successfully. Anything different or difficult, we want to pass that over to the other side.

Although I have a much more "hands on" situation with the defensive assistants than the offense, that doesn't mean I don't know what the offensive plan is or have some ideas on how it could be improved.

During the game I am constantly aware of the next play that is being called. If there is a time out and the quarterback comes over to talk to the coordinator, if it's a really critical down coming up I want to be right there and hear what they are going to suggest. That's part of our game plan. That's why the whole staff is involved.

We also try to lay out every situation in advance. And we prepare three options for every tough situation. That goes for 1st and 10, 2nd and 10, 2nd and 5, 2nd and 3, and so on. And for the various places on the field, for the various amounts of time left in the game, and for the score of the game.

Obviously, we will do something different on the opponent's 35 yardline with a minute left and trailing by four points than we would if we were on our own 15.

Those decisions are made ahead of time. They are thought out. That way such a decision won't be made hastily under the pressure of the game on the basis of emotion.

Now we get into one of those situations in a game. It's really nut-cutting time. We call time out and the quarterback comes over. These are the three options we have. I want the quarterback to hear them. I want him to pick if he has a favorite. If the quarterback says, "Coach, I really like the sprint out instead of the drop back in this situation," then we'll just about always go with the quarterback.

If he says he doesn't have any preference, then we'll go back and let the coordinator make the choice. He is up in the press box. That's what will happen, unless I have a strong feeling for one of the other options.

It might seem that we put more stock in what the quarterback wants than most coaches. The truth of the matter is that with an audible system, he can check off to something else anyway. Most quarterbacks wind up calling more of the game than you might think. Especially now with the one-back alignment we use. When we're one-back and spread out all over the field, there are some defenses we just can't block for certain plays. We haven't got enough people in the right places. So we have to get into color schemes and schemes that throw quick to somebody who is going to be open.

The quarterback knows that on some plays a certain receiver is going to be free. And that the ball has to be delivered right now! That's one of the things I think we're doing a better job of — our blitz pickup is vastly improved.

I do think there is a correlation between having a good week of practice and playing a good game, although I seldom refer to that in an after-game press conference. In fact, I would be much more likely to say we had a good week of practice after a defeat — in other words saying it wasn't a lack of preparation or effort that caused the loss but rather the good play of the opponent.

I can think of only one time in my 16 years that we had a "losing" week of practices. And it just drove me up a tree. I even ran the players off the field one night I was so sick and tired of looking at them.

That was in '82, the week before we lost to Washington State — a defeat that cost us a Rose Bowl invitation. We were not even in a game in which we were about a six touchdown favorite. Well, maybe not that much. But it was just awful.

I talked about that game earlier. I certainly don't need to dwell on it again.

My philosophy of developing a game plan is more like what we did at Michigan than at Florida State, where the emphasis was on the pass.

I thought we had a better balance between run and pass at Michigan. At Florida State the scales were tipped in favor of the pass. It was the correct philosophy no doubt as we went into so many games as underdogs. At Colorado, the scales were tipped to the run. There, we just had more running talent.

I thought we balanced it out a little better at Michigan. And that's the philosophy I've tried to maintain here at Washington. I recognized the fact that you've got to be able to run the football and play good defense to win, but I feel like we've got to have balance because we're still only going to go into half a dozen games as favorites. Many of the defensive teams we play are going to be as good or better than we are.

There are games, of course, where you sit back and critique it later and say, "Our productivity out of the run was terrible so we should have thrown more." Or, "Our passing was poor so we should have run more." But, hopefully, I have enough input during the game so that shouldn't happen. We should be able to make the necessary adjustments during the game.

Our staff meetings, which start each morning at 7:30, aren't solely devoted to devising a game plan. First we have a personnel meeting. We talk about the players on both sides of the ball and those involved in the kicking game. And we always talk academics, study table, tutoring. We also always have a recruiting report from Dick Baird, our recruiting coordinator. He's there every day to tell us what phone calls need to be made, what has to be written to certain prospects. Then we lay out that day's practice. We also critique the practice from the day before.

There are a myriad of things to do. I leave when the staff agenda for the day has been covered. A portable wall divides the room and the two staffs — offense and defense —continue to work on the practice plan and also on their game plan for the upcoming opponent.

The more time we spend as a group, talking about things that don't apply to everyone in the room, the more time we are wasting. It kills me to have people disorganized or unprepared. It's just like going out to practice. Some coaches have four-hour practices. I want to go out and get everything done in two hours that it takes them four.

The game plan begins with a "script" for our opening offensive series. We will take our basic formations that we've got ready for the game — three wide outs, one back, two tight ends, two wide outs, double flankers.

We'll take the basic plays for those formations and script some runs and passes to see how the opponent is going to cover them — how they're going to line up against those various formations. We might script the first 12 plays. It varies.

Sometimes, of course, you get chased out of the plan because of the situation — where you are on the field. But pretty early in the game you've got to be determined. We know what the opponent's game plan has been. Now we've got to determine what their game plan is for us.

So, during the first half I also want to know what new plays they've come up with for my defense to contend with, what new pass routes, what new formations.

We try to adjust and counteract to those changes as the first half goes along. But its at halftime that we actually have the opportunity to put it up on the board, to look at it and say to the players, "Okay, these are the adjustments. We tried to do these things on the field, but now this is what we've got to do in the second half."

We change some blocking. We change some coverages. Another thing, we try to zero in on what we want to do in the second half. What has been working for us in the first half? How do we expand on that success?

We tell them, "We put in all these plays for this game. But, in the first half, these four running plays were the best four. And these three passes. So, let's forget all the other stuff and let's go out and run those seven plays." The same thing defensively. "They're not throwing over there because of all our strong crashes. They're throwing over here. So we've got to run more weak blitzes." Or, "We can't seem to hold up man-for-man so we're going to play more zone." Those are the kind of decisions you can make at halftime.

Some coaches are obviously better at making halftime adjustments than others. Their teams are often tougher to handle in the second half. Other coaches tend to just go in the dressing room and scream and holler. Occasionally, if you're really mad at a team, because they were a four touchdown favorite and they're just out there slopping around, you can yell a little.

But, basically, my approach is that we've got to help the players at halftime so they can do a better job in the second half. Screaming at them isn't going to help. If they played real bad they already know that. We can mention it, but we've got to show them how to do better. That's when players really start to believe in their coaches. When you give them tips that will make them better. They want to win. You've got to come up with the ideas that will help them become more effective.

I put our whole game plan on a card. One side offense, the other for defense. Also included are all the combination of numbers as to whether we will go for one or two after a touchdown.

By the Thursday before each game I have made the decision, for instance, based on the score of the game and the time remaining and the yardage we must gain to make a first down, whether on fourth down we will go for it or kick a field goal. Then, if that situation arises, I'm not swayed by the emotion of the moment. The decision, based on calm thinking and the facts, has already been made.

Those decisions can change from game to game. We have played teams where we feel in advance that three-pointers aren't going to beat them. We need sevens.

While the normal rule of thumb might be that if it's fourth-and-one or less we'll go for it, otherwise we'll kick the field goal, for this particular game we might push that back to fourth and two.

I have a philosophy that says if we get to the other guy's 15 yardline we must score. You give your opponent a great psychological lift if you get down close and don't get anything out of it.

We go back to that yardage thing again. If it's fourth and two or three and it's within range of our kicker, we're going to settle for the field goal.

Which brings us to another key issue. Are we going to go for a win or a tie. That's the hardest decision of all. But we want to make the decision on Thursday, not in the heat of battle. And make it based on where we are in league play and who we are playing and what a tie or victory or loss will mean to us.

As long as we are in the race and undefeated, we're going to go for a tie. We're talking about the last drive of a game. If you lose a game in league play, you may be forced to go the rest of the season saying, "Must win." You can't consider going for a tie. You may need a victory late in the season to get an invitation to a bowl game.

We have lost games because we were gambling out of our end zone with the score tied because we felt we had to win to get a bowl game.

Also, sometimes, when you go for a tie you lose ground with the players and the fans. We played UCLA out here a few years ago and it was a "must win" game. More to salvage a decent season than anything else. We were out of the race. We had started the final drive on our three or four yardline. Just had a couple of minutes to go. And our players took it all the way down.

When they got down there, it was the one time that I ever changed my mind. I felt it was better for us to tie UCLA and give our players some satisfaction than to throw the ball into the end zone on fourth down and lose. So I had them kick the field goal for a tie.

Even a game plan can't be etched in stone.

chapter twenty five

Realistic dream or not,
many college athletes
have the NFL as a goal

A major college football coach has to know that
many of his scholarship athletes come to school with
the primary goal of becoming an NFL player.

We all hope that the opportunity for an expense-
paid college education is important to the athlete. And
we strive to see that he gets it. The experience of playing at the major college level and the many valuable
lessons to be learned are things which they will remember for years to come.

But the truth is that the vast majority of our players dream of the chance to play in the NFL. They
know the odds are against them reaching such a goal.
But, from the moment they step on the campus, that is
their dream. It is comparable to a drama student
dreaming of becoming a great actor or a music major
dreaming of playing at Carnegie Hall.

I may be in the minority among coaches, but I
think it's one of my responsibilities to help them fulfill
that dream.

The high school recruit has one other major desire — that he'll play at the major college level with the varsity as a freshman. It's amazing how many kids pick a school because a college recruiter convinces him that he will start as a freshman. I don't know how you could ever tell a recruit that he will start.

We don't hard sell the idea that a recruit will get playing time his first year. But we certainly point out that some of them have. We tell a recruit that he'll get a chance — an opportunity — to make it as a freshman.

We point out that Jacque Robinson was the MVP of the Rose Bowl as a freshman. So was Paul Skansi in the Sun Bowl in 1979. Willis Ray Mackey, a Texas native, scored the winning touchdown against the Longhorns in that same Sun Bowl game when he was a true freshman.

So, we tell them it can happen. If they are good enough, we're going to play them.

I will not redshirt any player who can help the team win. That's the bottom line. That goes for the first game of the year or the last game of the year. If he can help, he's going to play.

Freshmen at every school start at the bottom and work their way up. Once they get up to the third team, because of the restriction on the size of the travel squad, you have to consider them for play on the special teams.

If you work your way up to our third team, then we're going to sit down with you and find out whether you'd like to play some special teams this year or would you rather not do that and save the year — redshirt.

If they get up to the second team there is no decision to be made. They're going to play.

We've told freshman quarterbacks who we — and they — would like to redshirt, that if he gets up to the third team — we take three QBs on the road — that he'll do everything in practice. He just won't play. But we tell him, "If we need you in the 10th or 11th game, or the bowl game, you're going to play."

The answer I get from third team freshmen varies. We had a running back a couple of years ago named Tommy Smith. I told him we could guarantee him second team status as a strong safety if he wanted to switch over to defense. And also, on defense, he would get some playing time on the special teams.

Tommy had played both ways in high school and we knew he could be a backup defensive back with very little practice time. The opportunity came about because of an injury to a starter.

The problem was, and we told him, "When the other guy gets well and comes back, you'll be bumped down to third team and may not see any more action."

But he wanted to play. We put him in and he blocked a punt in his first college game against USC and scored.

Changing positions, even from one side of the ball to the other, is not all that unusual. Every recruit has a position idea. I tell them, "Some coach is going to promise you that you're going to be a starter for him at left guard or right tackle or inside left linebacker.

"I've been in this game 30-some years and I look at your video tape and I think I've got some idea of what your potential is. But once I see you for a year or two, then I'm going to know for sure and I'm going to try to project you into the NFL. I'm going to try to pick the position where you can make it as a pro.

"When you come in, I'm going to let you play the position you want to play. If I want to move you, I'll bring you in and we'll talk about it. It'll be a move to help the team and also to give you the chance to play sooner. The first move, if one is made, is to give you the chance to play sooner. If we move you again after that, it will be so you've got a better chance of playing in the NFL."

Mark Jerue would never have made it in the pros as a
225-pound middle guard, but had a fine career with the
LA Rams as a linebacker.

As I said earlier, I'm certainly aware that the majority of the players have the NFL as their No. 1 goal when they come to college, especially those who are heavily recruited by the major football schools.

A few don't. They just want to get their education. They have their career goals in mind. But "most" is a fair word to use. Most of them are aiming at becoming good enough to play in the NFL.

We put a lot of academic emphasis on them throughout their career. We tell them, "A lot of you guys want to go to the NFL, but not very many of you are going to make it. Just look at the number of new players who make it each year."

As a coach, I have to keep beating down the goal of becoming an NFL player. There's nothing wrong with the goal. But you've got to get the academic goal in there too. Sometimes you have to be a little negative to get the academic goal sold. We want them to get a quality education so they will have something to fall back on if they don't make it in pro ball.

We tell them, "Look at the seniors you played with last year. How many of them got a chance in pro ball and how many of them made it?"

Back to position changes. On the other side of the coin, I can name a number of players we have moved, even up into their senior year, who wound up with extended NFL careers because we gave them the opportunity to change positions in college.

Mark Jerue was an MVP in the Rose Bowl as a middle guard. But he weighed about 225 pounds. That was fine for college ball. In fact, he would still be a good middle guard. He had great quickness. Just a fine football player.

But we couldn't generate any interest in the NFL. The scouts would come by and say, "He's too small. He can't play."

So, I called him into the office the spring before his senior year. I basically said, "Mark, this is what I think.

Anthony Allen:
From quarterback to wide receiver to the NFL.

No. 1, you'll be a great middle guard for us next fall, and a team captain. And I'll be satisfied with that.

"No. 2, however, if that also satisfies you, the NFL isn't going to take you as a defensive lineman. They think you're too small. And, No. 3, I think you can make it in the pros as a linebacker. What I propose is that you go out this spring and play inside linebacker. We'll spend the spring doing that. If it doesn't work, you can go back to middle guard and still be a starter. It won't hurt you, and it may open up the opportunity to play pro ball."

And it did. He played a long time with the Rams.

Another was the case of Anthony Allen. He had been a high school quarterback. When he got here he wasn't all that excited about playing quarterback, but we had some quarterback problems because of injuries. We needed him there, so Anthony was a quarterback his first two years, although we managed to redshirt him one of those seasons.

Then I called Anthony in and said, "Okay, you've helped the team for two years playing a position that you won't be able to play in the NFL. Although you could be a good college quarterback, you're not tall enough and your arm isn't strong enough to make it as a pro. I'm going to give you the option now of switching to wide receiver or cornerback. You can stay at quarterback if you want, but I think you can make it in the NFL at either wide receiver or cornerback." Anthony decided to move to wide receiver after making a very astute observation. He said, "Well, coach, what if I we have another quarterback injury and I have to come back to that position again? If that were to happen, I'd be better to switch to wide receiver because then I'd still know the offense."

That's the switch he made. We didn't have to move him back to quarterback and he made it in the NFL as a receiver.

Doug Martin
A dozen seasons with the
Minnesota Vikings

Blair Bush
A long NFL career with
Cincinnati, Seattle and
Green Bay

When you consider that I felt Allen was too short for the NFL as a quarterback at 5-10 or 5-11, it's a good thing I played when I did. Nowadays, I certainly wouldn't recruit myself. Even at the college level not too many people are looking for 5-9 quarterbacks.

Some of the more notable pro players I've had here at Washington include Blair Bush, who played 13 years in the NFL with Cincinnati, Seattle and Green Bay; Nesby Glasgow, a cornerback on our 1978 Rose Bowl team, who spent an equal amount of time with the Colts and Seahawks; Doug Martin, the first in a series of great defensive tackles we had. He played a dozen seasons with the Minnesota Vikings.

Then there was Mark Lee, who is going into his 13th season with the Packers, and Mike Lansford, who had a great 10 years with the Rams. Dave Browning spent more than a half dozen season in the NFL as did Jeff Toews, Michael Jackson, Stafford Mays, Curt Marsh, Ray Horton, Vince Newsome, Paul Skansi, Chuck Nelson, Steve Pelluer and Rick Mallory.

Ron Homes was a No. 1 pick in the 1985 NFL draft and Joe Kelly was a first round choice in 1986. Reggie Rogers was a No. 1 in 1987 and Bern Brostek in 1990.

Since I came to Washington, we've had 90 players drafted, seven in the first round.

And that doesn't count Warren Moon, the first pro quarterback to exceed 5,000 yards in a season. He played in Canada for five years, where he helped Edmunton win five Grey Cup championships, before making it big in the NFL at Houston.

Some people think that we ought to let the talented athlete come to college and just "major" in football. That's not the proper solution, even though, if we are honest, all major college coaches have a few students who do not have a lot of interest in academics. It's very difficult for them. They struggle a lot in class because they don't have the skills that their fellow classmates have.

What you have is one group of kids who are willing to try to the very best of their ability and another group that is not willing to work. It's that latter bunch who fall by the wayside academically.

Sometimes, however, I think the finger is pointed unfairly at the athlete. What about the college student who has only one goal — to succeed on the New York stage? He gets into drama and does very little if anything else academically.

Or the talented trumpet player at the School of Music. He and the athlete are in much the same boat. He can't take trumpet lessons all day long.

The answer is that they both need to get a well-rounded education. And that's what we're into for the athlete. And I'm supportive of that approach.

chapter twenty six

Run-ins with the refs;
I'll get after them
if I think they're wrong

Earlier I talked about the time Bear Bryant went out on the field to point out an error the officials were making when they called an incomplete shovel pass a fumble.

The Bear got the ref to change the call, but then got slapped with a 15-yard penalty for coming on the field.

A coach has the right to have a conference with the referee at any time. But there is a procedure we have to follow. First, I have to call a time out. Then, if the officials turn out to be right — in other words, if they win the argument — I'm charged with the time out. If I win, it's charged to them.

I haven't done it very often. In fact, I can't remember the last time. If you do, you want to be pretty sure. If it's on a judgement call, pass interference, things like that, you can't get a reversal anyway.

Even though you can't do anything about a bad call on a situation like that, I still want to be vocal about it.

On the sideline, if I see it and I think they're wrong, I'll get after them. I'll yell plenty. If I don't see it — after all, field level on the sidelines is the worst seat in the stadium — I'll ask the guys in the press box if it was a good call. I want them to be honest. I don't want them to b.s. me.

If they say, "Coach, it was a poor call," then I'll get after the officials. I'll let them know.

The problem with our sport is you can't get at all the officials. In basketball, all three refs are right there. The coach can reach them vocally. In football you can only get to the two wing officials who are closest to you. The others can't hear you. I might ask the wing official to give a message to the guy who made the call. But they are primarily only obligated to give messages to the referee.

Of course, if one of the two on my side makes a mistake, I'm really going to let him know.

There have been times when I have seen things and got really mad. I can get angry, like anyone else, but I try to stay off the field. I know that will get a coach in trouble.

Oh, a time or two I've been guilty of being outside the coaches box. But, the officials have generally been very good. Since they know I'm not just a constant complainer, I've never been flagged for going outside the coaching box.

When I calm down I'll ask the official what he called so I'll know what to look for when I see the video.

In the Pac-10 Conference, we have a couple of policies governing coach-referee relationships which I think are very good.

First, we are not supposed to criticize the officiating publicly.

The second is that we have a system in the conference that if I don't like the job a certain official is doing,

I can "rest" him for a year or two — keep him from officiating our games.

Our officials are rated during each game by a spotter in the press box. That person is generally a retired, but very experienced official.

After each game our staff also evaluates and rates the officials. And we've got the advantage of the film. So we should do a good job and be as objective as we can. Not just rate an official down because we lost the game.

After a game is played, both coaching staffs should have similar ratings of the officials. That's if we are honest and objective.

But, if an official keeps getting a low score from us, we do have the right to keep him from working our games for a couple of years. And, if they continue to get low scores they would lose their officiating job.

The officials in our conference spend a lot of time working to get better. They have meetings all fall. And summer meetings. They work our spring practices. Really, for what they're getting paid, we're no doubt coming out of it way ahead.

The thing that has always bothered me about officiating is that a split crew has been used for the Rose Bowl. Half the officials have come from the Pac-10 and half from the Big Ten.

I just don't like that. I don't think it's fair to the Rose Bowl and I don't think it's fair to the officials.

Most of the bowls have gone outside the two leagues involved for some time. That way you get a full crew from a neutral conference that is used to working together.

Now we are going to finally have a similar setup for the Rose Bowl.

Two years ago, Michigan was in the Rose Bowl. It was Bo's last game. He had a fake punt play that went all the way for a touchdown. It looked like it was going

A pre-game conference with the referee will often alleviate problems later on.

to win the game for him. But it was called back. And Michigan lost.

Bo was really upset. And it was an official from the Pac-10 who made the call. I know the Pac-10 guy. He's going to call it the way he sees it. He isn't going to make the call just because it was Michigan. And I don't think any of the other officials would do that either. But, whether justified or not, you can get into that accusation of dishonesty. No matter what is said, the appearance of impropriety is there. And that isn't fair to the officials.

One of the strangest officiating situations I've ever been involved with came in our Orange Bowl game against Oklahoma following the 1984 season.

Oklahoma has always had this little wagon — they call it the Sooner Schooner — pulled by four small horses that races onto the field whenever they score.

Well, just into the fourth quarter, the score was tied at 14-14. As I remember, Oklahoma got down close but we held and on fourth down they had to settle for a field goal.

The kick appeared to be good to give them a 17-14 lead. And here came the Schooner racing onto the field in celebration. I think the ref signaled the field goal good, not having seen that one of the other officials had thrown a flag for Oklahoma being offside.

The refs couldn't get the wagon off the field and it caused a big delay. So, in addition to the five-yard penalty for offsides, they also penalized them for delaying the game and then Tim Peoples blocked the next attempted field goal and we took over on our own 24-yard line.

They felt like it changed the momentum of the game, although it didn't really affect the outcome. We beat them by 11 points, 28-17.

Naturally, the call pleased a large number of Husky fans and upset the same number of Oklahoma supporters. It is something that always seems to come up whenever that game is discussed.

My favorite officiating story is the one about the coach who was really riding an official. The ref had finally had enough. He told the coach that if he opened his mouth again he was going to walk off a 15-yard penalty.

The coach asked, "Can you penalize me for what I'm thinking?"

Taken aback a little the ref said, "No, I don't think I can."

"Well, then," the coach replied, "I'm thinking you're a lousy official."

chapter twenty seven

*Reviewing the early 1980s
and the tension caused when
the Seahawks job opened up*

The decade of the '80s, which featured 10 straight winning seasons — a string that now extends to 14 in a row — began in 1980 with a Pac-10 Conference championship and a rematch in the Rose Bowl against Michigan.

We repeated in 1981 with another conference title and completed a 10-2 season by beating Iowa in the Rose Bowl. One of the more interesting games that year was our 13-3 victory over USC on the windiest day by far that I've ever been involved in a football game.

Jim Murray of the LA Times wrote, "It was so windy that there were white caps on the johns."

As a matter of fact, the Evergreen Point Bridge was closed because of high winds and we had to drive the team bus around the Mercer Island Bridge to get to the stadium. It was a wet day with winds gusting to 60 miles an hours.

It's not often that a team can roll up only 120 yards in total offense against USC and come out ahead. But that's what we did.

Marcus Allen made college football history early in the game when he gained 13 yards on a sweep play to become the first player in college football history to reach the 2,000-yard pinnacle in a single season.

Our approach in that game was that Marcus would get his yards and that would be fine — because we couldn't totally stop him anyway — but our plan was to shut down the rest of their team. He made quite a few yards that day, 155 to be exact, but we held them to 41 yards passing and only 141 rushing as a team. The difference in the rushing total came from sacking their quarterback for some minus yards. So they had negative yards except for Allen.

That University of Washington team returned almost intact the next fall and we were ranked No. 1 in the 1982 pre-season poll. We remained No. 1 through seven straight victories, four of them in the Pac-10, before we lost to Stanford down in Palo Alto. Although we lost just one other game that season and finished 10-2 again after topping Maryland in the Aloha Bowl, we finished with a final ranking of No. 7.

Two weeks before the Stanford game, while we were still undefeated, the Seahawks fired head coach Jack Patera. Countless articles were being printed about whether or not Don James would become the new Seahawks coach.

Sportswriters were even going into bars and interviewing guys off the bar stools as to their thoughts on the subject. It was driving me nuts. There was a lot of speculation and it was proving to be a real distraction and disruption to our program.

Prior to the time Patera was fired, through our first five victories, we averaged 42 points a game and won them all handily. The week after they let Patera go, and all this speculation had started, we played Oregon

State in game No. 6. Although the final score of 34-17 sounded like we had another easy win, it was more of a struggle and closer than the score might indicate.

The longer the situation continued the more difficult things became. Game No. 7 was in Seattle against Texas Tech. And that was even tougher yet. We managed a narrow 10-3 victory.

By that time, another debate was going on in the newspapers. The writers started wondering out loud as to whether or not it would be right for the Seahawks, with owners who were Husky grads, to hire me away from the University of Washington. Or, if I should even take the job if it were offered.

Here we were rocking along as No. 1 in the nation. The week of the Stanford game, we were 7-0, and I felt a real need to put an end to all this speculation. So I sat down and talked it over with Carol.

I told her that my No. 1 belief is that in order to be really good at something you have to be dying to be doing it; and you have to be dying to be doing it at a particular place. It has never been a desire of mine to coach in the NFL, or coach the Seattle Seahawks. And, if the job were offered and I did take it, I would be taking the job more for the prestige, or the fame or the money. I was right where I wanted to be at the University of Washington.

During my entire career, to that point, my goals had been designed to be a college football coach. I was being named to national committees with the NCAA and the coaches association. I would be giving up all I had worked for if I took the Seattle job. I felt the need to end all speculation by taking my name out of the running at that time.

So I had a press conference at the airport before we left for Stanford. I said I was committing myself at that time to the University of Washington and I was not going to be a candidate for the Seahawks job and would appreciate it if that speculation would end. And we flew off to Stanford.

You'd think my announcement would have had a positive effect on our players, but Stanford played as good that day as anybody we've ever played. And they had John Elway. He was a great player. He was the best college quarterback I ever saw. Elway went 20 of 31 for 265 yards that afternoon. We were 9 for 19 with 3 interceptions. All together we had five turnovers.

They were beating us 24-17 at the half. We scored 14 points in the second half, but they got nine to make it 43-31. That broke our bubble.

Elway was a great scrambler with a great arm. We went into the game, with the idea that we couldn't play pass defense against him unless we contained him. We really worked our four front guys on keeping him in the pocket, and we did, but what that meant was that we won the containment battle but lost the war. We were so conscious of keeping him in the pocket and not letting him get to the outside that we didn't put any real pressure on him.

If you were to really fly in there after him, you might hurry him or you might flush him out. Then he would scramble. But, if you rushed with the No. 1 intent of not letting him escape the pocket, then you didn't get enough pressure and he'd just sit back there and pick your secondary to pieces.

If I were playing him again, I'd turn 'em loose and flush him if we had to, but make him run and/or complete the passes on the run. He was scary when he'd get out there. He'd find guys and get them the ball. When we contained him we didn't put any heat on him and he had a lot of time to throw. And you can't give Elway that luxury. I believe that most pro teams worry more about pressure than containment when they play against John now.

We came back to Seattle the next week and beat UCLA, then went on the road and beat Arizona State to get our record to 9-1.

Now we've still only got one loss and the conference championship is ours if we beat Washington State. But we went to Pullman and they beat us 24-20.

We had 390 yards in total offense, they had 286. We had 241 passing yards to their 44. Tim Cowan was 19 of 29. And the turnovers were even.

But we had a receiver who made his only fumble — not of that year but of his entire career — in that game. Our kicker, Chuck Nelson, missed his only field goal attempt of the year.

We also had two calls by the officials that cost us six points. I heard later that one of the officials apologized to the head of the Pac-10 officials that he had cost us the Rose Bowl.

One was the failure to call pass interference on a corner route when the defender tackled our receiver. The other was a pass completion in the corner of the end zone which he called out of bounds. We kicked a field goal on that one, so it only cost us four points. But the film later showed it was a completion.

That is probably the only time I blamed an official for contributing to a loss. But we played poorly. If we had played anywhere near our potential we would have won despite the officiating errors.

Prior to that game we were 9-1, ranked high and had the Rose Bowl in our pocket. And it would have been a third consecutive Rose Bowl. To make the matter even more difficult to swallow, WSU had a very poor season that year. They had only won two games prior to this, and ended up 3-7-1. It was a major upset and hurt us as much as any loss in my career.

You could almost see it coming. We had terrible practices the whole week before the game. And that's what happens when you have poor practices, poor preparation, poor coaching, poor officiating, and some

Plotting with Ken Driscoll on how to stop a UCLA drive late in the 1982 game against the Bruins. We did, winning 10-7.

players who had great careers making the only serious mistake of those careers in the same game.

It had been a sensational year for Chuck Nelson. He had made 30 field goals in a row. He had incredible accuracy. Then he misses one in the same game that Paul Skansi suffered the only fumble of his career. Some of our fans in the end zone were sure Nelson's kick was good, but that was not what the officials thought.

As a result, we ended up trading places with UCLA. They were scheduled to go to the Aloha bowl, but our loss put them in the Rose Bowl so we went to Hawaii. We played Maryland and Boomer Esiasen. It took a long time to get over the loss to Washington State. Even though we were in beautiful Hawaii, every minute of every day we were all asking ourselves, "Why are we here? We should be over there," meaning, of course, the Rose Bowl. At least we won the game, edging Maryland, 21-20.

We got to Esiasen. We hit him hard. I have never had so much respect for a player to come back and play the way he did in the second half. As it turned out, we had to come back with a last minute drive to win it.

Late in the fourth quarter, when trailing, we tried a fake punt from deep in our own territory that really was a disastrous play. It was fourth down and we didn't put the signal on correctly. Half the team thought a regular punt was coming up.

We have a signal that puts the play on, or takes it off if the punter doesn't think it is there. He decided to put it on, but he didn't tell the team. He was supposed to pass, but the receiver didn't even know the ball was coming. They took over on the 19 and it looks as though the game is over for us.

They already had their 20 points and we had 14, but after three downs they missed a 32-yard field goal and we took over the ball on the 20 with 3:49 left. We drove 80 yards in 16 plays. Twice Tim Cowan ran for a first

After a practice in Honolulu prior to the Aloha Bowl game against Maryland in 1982.

down on fourth down and found Anthony Allen on a
pass play on yet another fourth-down call. Three
fourth-down plays to gain a first down in one drive.

It was third down on the Maryland 11 with 12
seconds left when Cowan hit Allen in the left corner of
the end zone for a touchdown to tie the score. Nelson's
extra point kick gave us the 21-20 victory. Cowan's 33
completions and 363 yards in total offense were alltime
Washington records.

When we got back, we found that Rick Redman, a
Husky booster watching the game on TV in Seattle was
so discouraged and so mad at us when we aborted that
fake punt that he turned off his set in anger. He didn't
know we won the game until he read it in the paper the
next day. And he had missed one of the great drives in
Washington football history. Which tells you, don't
ever give up.

Again the next year, in 1983, we would have been
in the Rose Bowl if we had beaten Washington State.
But we lost to them in Seattle and went back to the
Aloha bowl again. This time we lost to Penn State.

To say the least, our fans weren't real pleased with
us when we lost to Washington State twice in a row. Especially since both losses kept us out of the Rose Bowl.
But we've won the last five meetings against WSU, so
we've overcome that discontentment a little bit.

The next year, 1984, was an interesting season. We
won our first nine games. In one of those, the Oregon
game, we only had three first downs, yet won the game
17-10. We scored on a punt return to go ahead 7-0. Oregon threatened four times in the second half but Tim
Meamber intercepted a pass to set up a field goal. Jeff
Jaeger's field goal, a 32-yarder, put him into our record
book with at least one three-pointer in 16 consecutive
games. Tim Peoples then broke through to block an
Oregon punt, Mike Gaffney fell on the ball in the end
zone for a touchdown. So, the defense accounted for

both touchdowns and put the ball in position for the field goal.

Our offense got three first downs. Oregon had 17. In total offense, we had 109 yards, Oregon 268. That's why it is a team sport — it was a win. A theme we often use says, "Isn't it wonderful what can be accomplished when no one cares who gets the credit."

We wound up 11-1 on the year after beating Oklahoma in the Orange Bowl.

It was a great year for our defense. We got a ton of turnovers that season. We got six from Northwestern in the opener, five more against Michigan back there before 103,000 fans and four against Houston in the third game. Later we got six turnovers against both Oregon State and Stanford. The high point came against Arizona when we got 10 turnovers — six interceptions and four fumbles recovered.

We were unbeaten through nine straight games. Then came USC down there. We only got one turnover that day. And we were denied a bid to the Rose Bowl again.

We finished the regular season with a win over Washington State to go 10-1, a game in which we got five more turnovers.

We were ranked No. 3 when we went into the Orange Bowl game against No. 2 Oklahoma. That night we got three more turnovers, giving us 53 in 12 games.

By beating Oklahoma, we wound up ranked No. 2 in the country with an 11-1 record. BYU was No. 1 after an unbeaten season. If Michigan had beaten BYU in their bowl game we'd have been national champs. But, that's the highest ranking in the school's history. As we all know, a national championship is an elusive goal.

chapter twenty eight

*Seeking speed instead of size,
the success of the early '80s
turned into a downward spiral*

The success we had enjoyed during the early years of the 1980s turned into a downward spiral by the middle of the decade. I didn't like it at all. According to my "fan" mail, the alums didn't like it either.

We had back-to-back Rose Bowl appearances in 1980 and '81; a pair of 10-2 seasons in '81 and '82; an 11-1 record, an Orange Bowl victory over Oklahoma and the No. 2 ranking in the country in 1984.

But we slipped to 7-5 in '85. After bouncing back to eight victories the next year, we returned to a seven-win season in 1987 then skidded to a 6-5 record in '88.

The 1985 season started with losses to Oklahoma State and BYU. The regular season ended with a loss to Washington State. We did manage to salvage respectability, however, with a victory over Colorado in the Freedom Bowl.

The 1986 season got off to a much better start. We swamped Ohio State, 40-7, and got after BYU. As I said

At the kickoff luncheon, prior to our Rose Bowl victory over Iowa to complete the 1981 season, I posed with Hawkeye Coach Hayden Fry. The others, from the left, are: Hal Coonlee, president of the Tournament of Roses; Mike Lude, my athletic director at both Kent State and UW; Bump Elliott, Iowa's athletic director, and Bill Nicols, Rose Bowl representative.

earlier, we owed them one after they beat us out of the No. 1 ranking in '84. We beat them, 52-21.

Our only losses were to USC and Arizona State, while the UCLA game ended in a 17-17 tie. We beat all the Northwest schools plus Cal and Stanford and stood 8-2-1 going into a Sun Bowl game against Alabama.

If there was any one factor that led to our skid the next two years it was that bowl game. The biggest problem we had in playing Alabama was that we just didn't have enough speed to stay with them.

After that game we decided that we had been worrying too much about recruiting size instead of speed. As a result, before we would even go after a potential recruit, we felt like we had to really know his true speed. If we questioned his speed — couldn't get what we thought was a legitimate time on him — we would drop him from our list.

There was one major problem, however. There is not a high school coach in America who doesn't know the number to say when a Division 1A college coach asks him how fast his receiver is.

Some of the guys who are really 4.8 or 4.9, the coach is going to say 4.6. They want to help their kids get a scholarship and we're not allowed to time them or try them out in any way. And we got caught up in too many speed mistakes.

We'd like a young man on film. He looked good. And his coach says he runs 4.6. We just had too many people giving us misinformation. If you can't run, you can't play. Despite putting all this emphasis on going after speed, because of the misinformation we accepted we became too slow as a team during the next couple of years.

We recruited a lot of good kids, but they couldn't run fast enough to compete for a championship. And that was the start of the downward spiral.

During that period of time we also made some other recruiting mistakes. I can think of four or five players who wanted to come, but who we rejected or dropped. Yet they became very good players for somebody else. I'm talking about all-conference type players. And a couple of them are still in the NFL.

I'll also never forget the case of another player who is now in the NFL. One of my coaches rejected the idea of even starting to recruit him. He was from a local high school, 6-7, 235 pounds and playing all sports. His high school coach finally came to me at a clinic I was conducting and said, "I really think you're missing the boat on this kid."

But I hear that a lot.

However, the more he told me about him the more excited I got. The coach told me the young man was playing basketball at his school that night. So Carol and I went down and watched him play. I watched his movement and I couldn't believe we weren't recruiting him.

We tried to make a late run at him, but by that time he was discouraged that we hadn't shown any interest early on and we lost him.

We did too many of those things during that stretch of time. We were making bad decisions — taking guys who were inferior and rejecting prospects who wanted to come and who turned out to be better than the ones we took.

Later, the recruiting got straightened out and we also changed the work ethics. We had a team meeting and talked about turning things around and what we needed to do.

Looking back on that period of time in a little more detail, we were 6-4-1 before beating Tulane in the Independence Bowl to finish 7-4-1 in 1987, the year after the Sun Bowl loss to Alabama.

Mack Brown was the coach at Tulane, but he had already accepted the North Carolina job before our bowl game. That gave us an edge. They were a good throwing team. They had knocked off LSU that year.

Brown had done a great job at Tulane but could not overcome the disruption caused by the coaching staff change.

The next year was the no bowl year. We were 6 and 5. I don't like to dwell on a year like that. It was the only season without a bowl in the last 12. But it is an interesting year to look back on.

We started with victories over Purdue, Army and San Jose State. After losing to UCLA, we bounced back to beat Arizona State and we're 4 and 1. Then, at the end of the game against USC, we could have kicked an extra point for a tie, but we went for two and lost 28-27.

Before the season was over we lost to both Oregon and Arizona by three points each and ended the year with a one-point loss to Washington State. So, four of our five losses that year were by a total of eight points.

We were not all that good a football team, but you would have thought the world had come to an end around here. We had gone from 11 wins the year we beat Oklahoma in the Orange Bowl and were ranked No. 2 in the country, to eight wins, then seven and now six.

The fact that four of the five losses were by a total of eight points didn't mean much.

The main instruction I got when I first came to Seattle was "just be competitive." Here we were very competitive. But that was no longer good enough.

We were not any more pleased with the won-loss record than the fans. In addition, we were ranked 10th in the league in rushing defense, which is not at all typical of our defense.

What was so amazing, however, was the fact that there weren't any lynch parties out after me. Oh, there were a lot of innuendos and insinuations. And the media got all caught up in the 11, 8, 7, 6 business. The theme of the writers was, "They're going the wrong way!" and "They can never bring it back."

If not the alums, the media had the call out to re-place some coaches. All the things that you hear under circumstances like that. People were not satisfied, but more importantly the players and coaches were not pleased and we did something about it. I think we've brought it back real well in the last two years from the standpoint of competitiveness, speed and toughness.

In '89 , after winning our first two, we lost three in a row. But we recovered real well and only lost one game in our last seven. That got us back in a bowl game and we beat Florida, 34-7, in the Freedom Bowl. That was a great bowl victory.

We regained a lot of confidence in the closing weeks of the season by beating Oregon State, 51-14, and Washington State, 20-9, in addition to the bowl game.

Our quarterback in the bowl game was Cary Conk-lin. Emmett Smith was on that Florida team. But that was again a coaching staff that was changing. Florida's interim coach was Gary Darnell and we jumped out to 27-7 halftime lead.

We wound up with 433 yards in total offense to just 231 for Florida. So we had a good game on both sides of the ball. Greg Lewis, who was our tailback again this past year, had 97 yards.

It made a good ending for the year and gave us some momentum leading into 1990, a season that was climaxed by our Rose Bowl victory over Iowa. We'll re-view that in more detail next.

chapter twenty nine

*The Centennial game victory
over Southern California
was a key to success in 1990*

We opened last season against San Jose State. It was a touch and go struggle. They played as well as we did, and they went on to have a good year. San Jose beat Stanford and barely lost to California by a point or two. They won their league. But we got a win against them.

After that we went back to Purdue and got another victory. It was Fred Akers' fourth year and Purdue was a much improved team.

Then we had USC in our Centennial Game. It was certainly THE game of the year. There were a lot of big parties. Former players and coaches were back. Fortunately, we didn't do anything to dampen the spirit of the weekend. We blanked the Trojans, 31-0.

Then we went out to play eventual national champion Colorado on the road. The game started out okay and we scored early. But in the middle of the game they had three straight drives where they scored.

At the end of the game we came back and got down to their 7-yardline with 50-some seconds left. We threw four passes, two of which were in our receiver's hands in the end zone but were dropped. We lost, 20-14, but could have won it with a touchdown on that last drive.

But the players gained a lot of confidence from the Colorado game. We felt Colorado would be the most physical team we would play, and they were.

So, after that game, we came out and really started getting after people. We beat Arizona State, Oregon, Stanford, California and Arizona in order. And we piled up some big scores during that stretch.

Now we were 8-1 and unbeaten in Pac-10 play. In fact, the league championship was all locked up after the win against Arizona. We had two games left in the regular season but we'd already cinched the Rose Bowl.

We were ranked second in both polls and figured if we could win the last three — UCLA and Washington State plus the Rose Bowl — we'd have a real shot at a national championship.

So here comes UCLA to Seattle. It was a real windy day and they had a good game plan. They were going to run the shotgun and throw the quick passing series. We had become a blitz team. We were sending people and blitzing quarterbacks. UCLA had decided to go to the shotgun and throw quick before we could get to the passer.

We were still doing okay until we called a strong safety crash early in the game. They hit a quick opener on us and we had no free safety to stop the ball carrier.

It was a bad call on our part. A strong safety crash should only be called against a tight end formation. Then the weak safety can get back and help in the middle. At least we should have had a checkoff to get us out of a bad call.

As it turned out, we had all the gaps covered, but they hit a fullback dive in there with a lead block on our linebacker and the guy ran straight down the mid-

dle untouched. He could have run all the way to Spo-
kane if he had wanted to. That touchdown gave them a
lead and kept them in the game the entire afternoon.

It was give and take all day. We actually even got
the lead in the fourth quarter, but then they put together another drive and got a pass to Scott Miller,
their wide receiver, in the end zone. Chuck Mincy, our
cornerback, thought he had the ball when they were
coming down, but Miller took it away from him, rolled
over and held the ball up for the officials when they hit
the ground. Touchdown!

That tied the score and then we threw an interception trying to come back and that put them in a position
to kick a field goal to win.

We did finish the regular season on a good note,
getting a great win over our arch rival, Washington
State. So, we wound up 9-2 going into the Rose Bowl
game against Iowa.

Iowa had three great victories on the road during
its regular season — Illinois, Michigan and Michigan
State. They were beaten by Ohio State at home, I think
on the last play of the game, and they lost their big rival
game to Minnesota.

As most teams, they were a little beat up at the end
of the season. But both teams went into the Rose Bowl
game fairly healthy. You usually get most players
healed up in that month between the end of the season
and the bowl game.

Things went real well for us. We blocked a punt
for a touchdown right away. They were going to try a
trick play and saw it wasn't going to work, that we had
it covered, so the kicker moved up close and Andy Mason got through in the middle and blocked the punt and
Dana Hall recovered it in the end zone.

Then we got a field goal. But Iowa came back with
a drive behind the running of Nick Bell. He's just
great. A 250-pounder with super speed. Bell scored to
make it 10-7.

Quarterback Mark Brunell was the MVP in our 1991 Rose Bowl win over Iowa.

After that, however, a whole series of things went our way. Charles Mincy intercepted a pass to score a touchdown and our offense really played well. It was like 33-7 at halftime.

We got through the third quarter okay, so I started to substitute. After all, you'd like all the players to have the thrill of playing in a Rose Bowl.

But, Iowa started moving the ball and scored a couple of times against our backup players. I learned from that game that their first team was better than our second. It's a tough thing to decide from the sideline when the game is over.

I've never been a coach to run up the score. I don't think it's good for football. It definitely doesn't help your team any. I can't understand why people think it does them a lot of good to leave a quarterback or tailback in just to run up big numbers. I think it's a poor way of getting recognition.

Anyway, the score got close enough that I put our offensive starters back in and they scored real quick on a touchdown pass form Mark Brunnell to Mario Bailey.

But Iowa scored again. In that stretch, they tried three onside kicks and got two of them back. So there were two possessions we lost. If we'd gotten those two on-side kicks, we would have run a lot more time off the clock and would have kept the score down some.

If we hadn't scored with the first team late in the game, on Iowa's last drive we would have been ahead by only five points instead of 12. That would have made things a little more exciting than I would have liked.

The onside kicks gave us fits. What happened in this case was that on Iowa's first one, we had a player who just froze. He didn't go for the ball. I guess he thought it was going to go out of bounds. One of their players stood in bounds and reached out and grabbed it.

On the second one, we didn't have enough guys at the spot of the kick and they had too many. You never know what happens down at the bottom of the pile before the ref gets there. One of our smallest receivers, Mario Bailey at 5-8 and 160 pounds, had it. At least for a while. He was our best receiver and we had him at the point of attack. But he didn't get any help.

As a result of all that action toward the end of the game, the final score was 46-34. It was the highest-scoring game in the 75-year history of the Rose Bowl.

It was our 11th bowl game in the last 12 seasons and improved our record to 9-3 against bowl opponents. Considering that a bowl game matches you against another team that has had a highly successful season, it's a record of which I'm proud.

chapter thirty

Working with your peers
is an important aspect
of any profession

The American Football Coaches Association is the governing body of my profession. I have always felt that if a person wants to have an influential voice in order to bring about change for the good — in any profession — he needs to volunteer his services to such an organization. Put something back, not just take.

I can remember going to my first convention as a graduate assistant from Kansas and seeing all the "name" coaches — such as Bear Bryant, Rip Engle, Bill Murray, Jim Tatum and others — and going to the "Coach of the Year" banquet.

I suppose I set a goal at that time of wanting to be up there on the dias some day. And, eventually it happened. Being named the Coach of the Year after the 1977 season and later being elected president of the AFCA certainly are two of the biggest highlights of my career.

I've been very fortunate to be up on the dias at the convention as a trustee, a conference champion, Coach of the Year and then as president.

My election as Coach of the Year by my peers capped our exciting 1977 season. That's when we came back from a 1-3 start to beat a great Michigan team in the Rose Bowl.

Fred Akers was undefeated and playing Notre Dame in the Cotton Bowl that same day. But Texas lost. He would have been Coach of the Year with a victory, but I got a lot of visibility out of our season and the Rose Bowl victory.

In addition to the official Coach of the Year plaque, I was given a second plaque with two Los Angeles Times newspaper stories engraved on it. They are a fun reminder of a game, probably more than any other, that helped us turn the corner and establish our University of Washington program into what it is today.

They may dredge up some pleasant memories for you as well. Bob Oates of the LA Times wrote: "At dusk on Monday, Washington's defensive team made two interceptions to win a game the Huskies astonishingly won with a lively quarterback, Warren Moon, and one of the most daring offensive attacks in the 64 winters of the Rose Bowl.

"Michigan's last two threats died with those interceptions at the Husky three and seven yard lines as Washington outplayed the Wolverines in a 27-20 upset before a crowd 105,312. Don James' Pacific 8 team came in as a two touchdown underdog and took it to Michigan's Big Ten champion with a crafty, sparkling offense that surprisingly opened leads of 17-0 at halftime and 24-0 in the third quarter.

"At that late hour, Michigan's veteran coach Bo Schembleckler and his friendly quarterback Rick Leach, decided to prove they really do have a pass offense. Abruptly launching a furious air attack, that was both well conceived and well executed, the Wolverines raced to three touchdowns in the last 20 minutes and started what looked for all the world like the game-tying drive until linebacker Michael Jackson aggressively intercepted for the Huskies at the three-yard line.

"Thirty-eight seconds later, with 40 seconds left, Washington cornerback Nesby Glasgow intercepted and Schmblechler had lost his fourth Rose Bowl in four visits. He is now 0-8-1 in the final games of his nine years at Michigan and the Pac-8 is now 8-1 in the last nine Rose Bowls. Since 1968, only Woody Hayes' Ohio State team has won for the Big Ten at Pasadena."

The other story on the plaque was written by Mark Purdy. He wrote: "Coach James said he had to gamble to win the game. So the Huskies spent the afternoon not only going for broke but risking bankruptcy on both offense and defense.

"We had nothing to lose," senior center Blair Bush said, "because it was the kind of thing where we were such big underdogs that even if we lost people would say, 'So what, they were supposed to lose.'

"At the beginning of the season, we had a goal to be here," added Husky quarterback Warren Moon, who was named the game's most valuable player. 'And we did it. We have confidence in everything we do.'

"In this case, that meant having confidence in an array of reverses, fake punts, and when in doubt, long passes. Moon had thrown for one touchdown and ran for two others. He was involved in most of the trickery.

"Warren has a lot of guts," James said, "and so does our offensive coordinator (Dick Scesniak). I got a little nervous when some of those plays were called down from the press box, (where Scesniak was sitting) but it was what we thought we had to do. It was not expected that we could hang in there with them head-to-head."

After serving on a variety of AFCA committees — I've been a member of the organization for 35 years now — I was chairman of the annual convention for three years. There was a lot of organizational work involved in that job, arranging for all the speakers and overseeing the many details involved.

It's an exciting convention because of the number of coaches who attend. All college coaches belong to the AFCA, from Division 1-A to the smallest junior college. And not just the head coaches. All the assistants are included. There are also allied members, such as ex-coaches and high school coaches. A lot of people attend. It's the event of the year.

As an organization we have accomplished quite a bit over the years. One of our main activities is lobbying for our sport. We get our ideas together and create legislation that we believe will be good for our athletes and coaches as well as for our great game of football.

Recently we reached an important goal by setting up a retirement trust for coaches. Frank Broyles and Bear Bryant tried this a number of years ago. But what they wound up with was basically an insurance program. It was not much different than what you or I could get at our place of employment.

We went to work as an association through our congressmen and senators and also did a massive lobbying job with all of our state legislators to get our plan approved. We received a tremendous amount of help and guidance from Larry Roseberry and his insurance company in getting our retirement program for our coaches.

Charlie McClendon, who had a distinguished coaching career highlighted by many years at LSU, is now the executive director of the AFCA. He'll have us fill out questionnaires that affect every part of our game — coaching, recruiting, rules, anything to do with the quality of our jobs. Then we'll discuss those things at the convention.

Another thing that Charlie Mac has gotten through recently is some temporary job protection for the assistant coaches when the head coach gets fired.

Since a new head coach is going to have the right to hire his own assistants, when a head coach gets fired, his assistants are normally going to be out of work.

The head coach may have one or two or even three years left on his contract. And he gets paid. But, since the assistants are on year-to-year contracts, they don't.

What we wanted to do was get our assistant coaches on fiscal year contracts rather than for the calendar year. If the head coach gets fired, it usually comes in late November or early December at the conclusion of a bad season. Being on a calendar year contract, the assistant coaches are looking at a last pay check coming in a matter of weeks.

If they were on fiscal year contracts, they would still be on the payroll for the rest of the school year — until June 30 — and that would give them a little breathing room, time to find another job.

The way it's been, with no money coming in, many assistant coaches have been forced out of the profession. Now, with his income maintained for awhile, he can take three or four months and work hard to stay in the profession by trying to relocate. He doesn't have to necessarily take the first thing that comes along.

It's surprising how much legislation comes up all over the country that affects our profession. We study it, then try to get our coaches to lobby their university presidents and athletic directors and work on what is good for our sport.

In order to raise some funds to help finance our retirement program, we developed the AFCA-sponsored Pigskin Classic, a pre-season game that is played in California. Colorado and Tennessee played to an exciting tie in the first game in August of 1990.

Because football provides the financing for the majority of the other sports at most schools, some people have proposed raising that income by adding a twelfth regular season game.

The Japan Bowl coaching staff for the January 1991 game.

From the left: Tom Mack, University of North Carolina; Yours truly; Joe Restic, Harvard; Forest Gregg, SMU; Fisher DeBerry, Air Force; Howard Schnellenberger, University of Louisville.

They will even point out that the pros play more
games than we do. Well, the pro players don't have the
demands of the classroom and studying. Eleven games
is surely sufficient, especially with two pre-season clas-
sics — the Kickoff and the Pigskin — and the bowl
games afterward. That's another reason we don't need
a playoff.

In addition to being named the Coach of the Year
by Kodak and the AFCA in 1977, I'm most appreciative
of several other coaching honors I've received over the
years.

There are several "Coach of the Year" awards
given each year. It is, of course, a great honor to be recognized by any of them.

After the 1984 season, when be beat Oklahoma in
the Orange Bowl and were ranked No. 2 nationally, I
was awarded the Woody Hayes Trophy and named the
Coach of the Year by the Touchdown Club of Columbus, Ohio. The same year I was given the Gold Helmet
Award in Seattle as the College Coach of the Year.

While at Kent State I won a Coach of the Year
award and that led to my later induction into the Tangerine Bowl Hall of Fame for having coached Kent
State to that bowl in 1972.

Another nice honor is having been named as a
coach for post-season, all-star games on several
occasions.

I have been a coach for the Japan Bowl two different times. That wasn't as difficult as it might seem
since the people who work with you speak English.

I've also done the East-West game a couple of times
and the North-South game in Miami when it was still
going. And the Hulu Bowl. They all are games that are
well organized.

The East-West game draws the biggest crowd. The
Shriners get behind it and you play before 80,000 people. They also take the game itself more seriously. The
teams practice longer and harder for that game.

In order to entice the players to go that far away, the Japan Bowl people really do a lot for the members of the teams. They entertain them, take them on tours and other outings.

Basically, they don't practice very much. They're not that worried about putting on an error-free game. They want a good game, an exciting game. But it's not that important that they go out and practice two-a-days for a week.

In fact, they practice twice for one hour each time and that is it. Then they play the game.

What you normally do in the all-star games is limit your plays and defenses. When you first get there you sit down with the other staff and the coaches all agree. You normally limit the offensive formations to two. You eliminate all shifting or man-in-motion plays.

Then you go to the defense and say, okay, you've got to stick with one defense. You can't stunt, you can't crash, you can't blitz. You're allowed two coverages against the pass. You play one zone and one man-to-man.

And you really cut back on the kicking game. You have to allow an onside kick in case the game situation would call for that. But you usually agree you're going to kick it off down the middle and that the receiving team will have one wedge return. You don't rush the punter, you don't rush the place kicker. That saves a lot of time in preparing the special teams. Besides, most of the players you get for an all-star game haven't played on special teams.

It's so simple you might have at the most a half dozen running plays. You can call them by holes or some people go into the game and just say sweep right, sweep left, off tackle right, off tackle left, trap or draw.

And you use just regular man-on-man blocking since you know where the defensive guys are going to be. You can put in a double team and a trap. Really

Greg Lewis: One of our best-ever tailbacks and the first recipient of the Doak Walker Award.

you try to set up the offense to make it an exciting game with more scoring.

That leads to more passing, which is just what the fans want to see. And you can call a hundred passes. The quarterback can direct the routes in the huddle, sending the guys wherever he wants. Like the sand lot days of drawing the plays in the dirt.

Speaking of all-star situations, when writing this book I was encouraged to pick an "all-James" team. That would be difficult. I could do it, but I'm not sure it would be fair to the many excellent players we've had at Washington.

Even if I were to pick, for instance, the 10 players I thought were the most outstanding in each area — 10 offensive linemen, 10 defensive backs, and so forth — the problem is that you wind up leaving somebody off. Especially the guy you've got on the list as No. 11. And people are bound to write in and say, "How can you leave so-and-so off, he's better than all of those you named." People ask mostly about the tailbacks we've had. The answer to that is the most productive tail-backs have been Joe Steele, Jacque Robinson and Greg Lewis. I don't think it hurts the rest of them for me to say that. I think everybody realizes that those three gained the most yards and played the most.

So let's just leave it at that.

chapter thirty one

*The NCAA rules change
so often that they are
difficult to administer*

George Raveling, the USC basketball coach, once said, "I wish the rules makers would just let us work with the rules for two years, then maybe we would understand them." I think this is a great idea as we have so many changes that it is hard to keep up.

Adhering to the myriad of NCAA rules regarding recruiting is a difficult task. The problem is compounded because there are so many people who impact your program. It's not just your own large staff, but it's the alumni.

Like all schools, we've got alums all over the world. They don't know the rules, yet we are held responsible by the NCAA for their actions. Even if an alum knew the rules at one time, the rules are constantly changing.

In a lot of towns, there might not have been a major college football prospect for the last 10 years. And what an interested alum could do in the way of contacting that prospect 10 years ago is likely not allowed today.

We have tried to organize what we call our "Husky Hunters". These are men who are really interested in recruitment from the standpoint of watching high school athletes play. We've tried to formulate a list and keep it updated and keep those people abreast of the rule changes. We have meetings and give them the new rules and also mail them out.

The problem for alums now is there is not much they can do. They cannot write or call a prospect, they cannot have personal contact with the player, on or off the campus. That really makes it cut and dried. That defines what they can — which is next to nothing — and cannot do.

We not only try to alert our alums but we also keep the players we are planning to recruit informed. As we start to recruit, the prospects have to know the rules. We encourage them to let us know if any of our alums violate any of the rules so we can contact the alum.

I've had recruits tell me that an alum did this or that because he didn't know it was against the rules. If it was wrong, we call the alum, explain that he can't do that and thus self-police ourselves. Generally, if we do a good job of that and self report the facts to the NCAA it is not considered a serious rules violation. You can hardly go through a recruiting season without having some things of that nature occur.

In the days before all the rule changes, schools would all but kidnap a kid the night before the signing so that no other school could get to him.

You not only couldn't do that under today's rules, there is now a moratorium. You can't even see a prospect for the last two days before signing. Next year the moratorium will last from two days before to three days after the signing date.

Since coaches won't be able to see a prospect during that time, we will have to go through the signing process by mail. Since coaches will lose total control of their letters of intent, that ought to be real exciting.

You can hand deliver the letter of intent, but you'll have to take it to him before the moratorium begins.

No telling what will happen during the intervening week. I obviously think it is a terrible rule, especially since we will only be permitted one phone call to the prospect each week.

The chaos that might result is scary. Let's assume we want to sign 18 recruits. You've got to put more than 18 letters out there. Some of your top choices are going to sign with some other school. Let's say you put 25 out since they must be in their hands the week before. One kid is committed, and then he suddenly backs out. So now you've got that letter in his home and he's not going to sign it. So, for that reason, you've got to have some other letters out.

I told the NCAA that I couldn't believe we are being asked to lose control of a $100,000 scholarship. If I'm coaching at a private school with high tuition., and I'm giving a kid a $20,000-a-year scholarship — which is basically $100,000 if he stays in my program for five years — are you telling me I've got to leave the letter in his home and he can sign it or not sign it and I won't know until it does or doesn't arrive in the mail a few days later?

The answer was yes!

What if I activate another letter and then the first young man changes his mind and signs my letter? Now I'm one over. You mean to tell me I've violated an NCAA rule because of that?

The answer again was yes. I think it's totally ridiculous.

But, regardless of what I might think, the rule goes into effect for the signing date in February 1992.

I don't know what we're going to do if we run into a recruit like we had this past year. He didn't want to get into a hassle with the recruiters from the various schools who were after him, so he just told each recruiter, "Don't worry, your school is my choice. I'm coming." Six different schools all thought they had him in the bag and counted him as one of their quota. Five of them, including us, were shocked when he signed with another school.

Under next year's rule, we might not find that out until our two or three top "backups" have given up on getting to go to Washington and have also signed with somebody else. Now, you not only don't get one of the 18 you were figuring on — in the hypothetical example I just used — but you don't get Nos. 19, 20 or 21 either.

We had one prospect I'll never forget. He changed his mind at least six times in the last couple of days. Another bizarre case occurred when we had a recruit from California on campus for his official visit. We had him staying in the University Towers Hotel. Yet a coach from another Pac-10 school — which shall go unnamed — came up to Seattle to keep his eye on the recruit. We found out he was even slipping notes under the door of the recruit's room while he was visiting our place.

Things are much better controlled now. The contact rule has really tightened down. That seemed like an unenforceable rule to a lot of people. They would ask, "How is the NCAA ever going to know if you contact a kid four or five times over a several month period rather than the allowable three?"

Well, the recruit himself is the big deterrent. If a school contacts him more than three times, and he's irritated because he doesn't want to go to that school, he may well turn the school in. Then they would really be in trouble.

I was on the NCAA football rules committee for six years. If I have a claim to fame for that service it was being instrumental in getting the penalty for pass interference changed from the spot of the foul to a 15-yarder — or less.

The pass interference penalty always bothered me. When I was in the Big Eight that was the big joke. If you wanted a long gain, throw a long pass. If you didn't complete it, you'd probably get a pass interference call.

In the time I was an assistant at Colorado I never saw so many pass interference calls.

It always bothered me, being a defensive backfield coach. First of all, when the ball is thrown it's a free ball. The defensive player has as much right to go after it as the receiver. Yet, at the end of the year when we tabulate all the pass interference calls, it's 95 to 98 percent against the defense.

I always felt there were more mistakes by officials in calling pass interference than any other call. And it is such a critical play. It could be a 45 or 50-yard penalty. Which translates into a 45 or 50-yard mistake. I've known coaches who actually lost games and lost their job because of an official's mistake in that kind of a situation.

I always wanted to get back to the way the play has been ruled at the high school level, a spot foul of up to 15 yards.

I tried and tried for years but couldn't get any support. Finally, BYU Coach Lavelle Edwards supported me. Lavelle was on the committee at the same time. He was an old defensive coach, too. He agreed with me and we got the rule changed.

The biggest question about the rule is the intentional foul. I know you're beating me on a deep pass so I just go ahead and tackle you. But we haven't seen much of that.

I really enjoyed my time on that committee and having some impact on the game. I was also on the committee when the use of the hands rules changed. For years offensive blockers had to block with closed fists while keeping their hands against their chest.

The pros taught an open hand approach and the hands were allowed to leave the chest area. At the time I was against the change and said, "Well, the cheaters finally won." I was a little disturbed at the time. But I think it's a lot better now. I don't know if there is any more holding or less. There is probably more but it is a lot easier on the officials.

It certainly has made protecting the passer a lot easier for the offensive linemen. My feeling was the quarterback shouldn't get protected if his linemen can't block. Now, of course, you can extend your hands and push with the open hands, as long as you keep them within the framework of your body and don't grab the defender's jersey.

The biggest complaint from the defensive coaches in trying to stop a proficient passing team is that they can't get to the passer because the offensive linemen are holding all the time.

There is no doubt about it, now that the hands are allowed to be open, the possibility of holding has increased. Before the rule change, the college line coaches were coaching what the pros were coaching. The defensive guys were hollering that it was illegal. And they were telling the umpire it's your responsibility to call it and stop it.

In reality, of course, it was up to the coaches to stop it by changing what they were teaching their players to do. But they never did. So then the college rule was changed to the pro rule.

Regarding offensive holding, we've got a new rule for 1991. The penalty will now be marked off from the point of the infraction instead of going back to the line of scrimmage. If I'm pass protecting blocking five yards back of the line of scrimmage, it's going to be 10 yards from that spot, or in reality a 15-yard penalty, not 10.

I think you just have to expect a certain amount of holding. If the hands are going to be out, they're going to grab a jersey. If we can keep the guys from tackling the defensive lineman, we will have made some progress.

I have always attempted to be a student of the rules. I felt I should know them. If I am going to criticize an official for making a bad call, I'd better be sure of what the rule says. I am still one of the few coaches who goes to the officials meeting that they have every August. I want to get the interpretations and how the officials are going to call things. Then I can make sure our coaches and players knew them as well.

I was also chairman of the recruiting committee for the NCAA. We basically discussed everything to do with the recruitment of college athletes in all sports.

We tried to make the rules more liveable and think in terms of the high school athlete, but also make the process more realistic for those of us who were out in the trenches, who had to deal with the recruit and the schools.

We were trying to make it easier on the high school athlete and more realistic in our evaluation process. A recruiting mistake is a costly mistake. If you give a scholarship to an athlete who can't play, because you didn't have enough time to evaluate him, you've made an expensive mistake.

The more time I can spend with a prospect the more I'm going to learn about him. I might have three visits and be sold on the young man. Yet, with a fourth or fifth visit find that he's not going to fit in. There are so many things you can learn with a little more time. That's the thing that bothers me about the rules we now have. We have restricted ourselves more now than ever.

Our scholarship for an instate player is worth around $6,000. For an out-of-state athlete it's $10,000. If we've had sufficient time to evaluate and get all the checks we want on character, athletic ability, academic transcripts and test scores — if we then make a decision to recruit the guy and make a mistake, it's nobody's fault but our own. But if we are forced to make that decision without the benefit of all the facts, then the rules can be blamed.

We also face another big recruiting change. This year, as in the past, we can continue to award as many as 25 scholarships in any one year, but can't have a total of more than 95 on scholarship at any one time. But the 95 number is about to drop. The next recruiting class will be down three to 92, then four more the following year to 88, and then down three more to 85 the year after that. We will lose 10 scholarships over a three-year period. The number you can take in any one year will stay constant, but the total number you can have on scholarship will drop.

At least here, in a metropolitan area, we can get kids on our campus. You can talk to them as much as you want on your campus. We can get them to games, have them come by to watch spring practices. As long as they come on their own and pay their own expenses, there is no limitation on that.

But, if you coached at a Kansas State or a Washington State, how many kids can they get to drive to out of the way places like Manhattan or Pullman?

I think the people who are in the metropolitan areas will have a big advantage. And there are some who are in much bigger population centers than we are in Seattle.

That's the problem with a lot of the NCAA legislation. It enhances things even more for those who are already in good shape.

When a coach does break the rules and gets caught, some people complain that he gets the school on probation, but then just leaves and gets a job somewhere else, leaving the original school with the problems.

There has been conversation at the American Football Coaches Association level of having the sanctions against a coach carry over with him should he go to another school.

That's the only way to make the sanction effective. It's obvious that most of the time, when a school is punished, that players are punished who weren't even involved in the infractions. A lot of times, the infractions occurred two, three or four years prior to the time they were either discovered or penalized for.

I think it is only fair that if a coach leaves the school for another institution, the sanctions should go against the coach. But I don't know if that's ever going to happen.

It remains the school's responsibility. The school would still be on probation, which isn't going to help the innocent kids who come along four years later.

The possibility of a national college playoff is another NCAA matter which is constantly in the news. Personally, I hope we never go to a playoff system at the major college level.

I look at it in two ways. First, I think the best way to look at it is from the player's standpoint. There are already so many demands on the players right now. We have fall camp, winter conditioning programs and spring practice, plus summer programs for them to follow. Then an 11-game season.

It's true that a playoff system would generate a lot of money, but I don't think you should do it unless there was some way for the players to get something out of it. At least get them the "laundry money" I had as a player. But I don't think that is going to happen.

I see what our players go through. We used to end up every year with Cal, USC, UCLA and Washington State as the last games on our schedule. You get your big games at the end. The players's level of concentration on football is at a peak. As a result, academics suffer.

Then there is the injury factor. We bang up kids in practice. And the season, by that time, takes its toll. They just don't need a longer season. It's long enough now.

We had a half dozen players who couldn't have competed for another six weeks after they got through playing Oklahoma in the Orange Bowl after the 1985 season. We had one player who had major knee sur-

Ron Holmes: A bowl game injury against Oklahoma would
have kept him from seeing action in a playoff.

gery. He was hurt during preparation for the game. There was another, Ron Holmes, who had a knee hurt in the game. The strong safety, Jimmy Rodgers, had to have surgery on his hand.

After beating Oklahoma we would have been one of the teams in a playoff, yet wouldn't have been anywhere near as strong as we would have been a few weeks earlier.

I also favor the bowl system. I think the bowls have done a lot for college football. Last year, colleges received over $60 million from the bowls. The Rose Bowl has meant a tremendous amount for the Pac-10 and Big Ten. Revenue sharing has kept a lot of the teams alive. A $500,000 check ever year, whether you're in the Rose Bowl or not, means a great deal.

I also like the fact that if we have 38 teams in bowl games, half of that number goes back home a winner. That gets us away from the mentality of professional sports where there is only one winner and everybody else is a loser.

I have talked to a lot of Division I-AA and Division II and III coaches — where they have playoffs — and they shudder at the demands of going back out for the extra games.

Regardless of what most people think, especially those in the media, I don't think playoffs at the major college level have a prayer.

I know that the money generated by a playoff would be huge. But, I think we're sending the wrong message if we were to have a playoff system just for the dollars. Especially if the participants don't get something out of it.

The university presidents are trying to send a message that there is an overemphasis on major college sports. And that they're going to do something about it. In my opinion, if they then allowed a playoff they would just be defeating everything they've tried to get established.

chapter thirty two

Are the universities
exploiting the athletes?
Plus, dealing with the media

Most of the stories you read in the newspapers about college athletics, particularly those dealing with the schools playing so-called bigtime football, would have you believe the players are some kind of underpaid slaves who are being exploited as they bring in millions of dollars at the gate.

I would like to see the rules permit a few benefits to the players which are not now allowed, but many major school programs — and I'm proud to count the University of Washington among them — are doing an outstanding job of making sure the athlete has the opportunity to get the education he deserved to receive when he came to college. I'm also here to admit that we have young people who are failing to take advantage of this great opportunity.

And, with the cost of a college education being what it is today — when you count in full tuition, books, fees, plus room and board — the scholarship player is getting a great value in return for his athletic talent.

I would agree that a football player is being exploited if it is not possible for him to get his degree because of the way the program is being run. They work long hours. They have night meetings and they are forced to take courses just to remain eligible.

If the school doesn't provide him support with tutoring, study table and counseling; if they won't let a player take a lab course because it occurs in the afternoon and keeps him from practice, then he is being exploited.

In past years, that kind of thing may have happened. But I think it's a rarity today. I know we, at the University of Washington, do everything in our power to see that our players get their degree. We have a post eligibility aid program. We have money available so a player can continue his studies after his playing days are over.

That's one of the major complaints we coaches had for years. But there wasn't anything we could do about it. It was an NCAA rule. When your eligibility was up, you were out of school. Then the NCAA made it permissible to give post-eligible assistance.

Although I am proud of the job we try to do, I'd have to admit that our graduation rate isn't as high as I'd like. We do, however, graduate a better percentage than the general college student population where only 32 percent ever graduate.

I don't think any coach can say his graduation rate is where he wants it. You hear of some who are in the 90 percent area, but I'm not sure that's realistic. Some schools figure their percentage in different ways.

Are they talking about those who sign as freshmen, or are they talking about those who stay with you until they are seniors. A fair way to evaluate the graduation rate of athletes would be to compare them to the non-athlete graduation rate.

With the rules we have now, there is no reason why a player shouldn't graduate. Unless, of course, he goes out early to the pros after his third year.

Every athlete must now have a declared major by the end of his second year. And they have to pass 36 quarter hours or 24 semester hours in their major by that time to play the next year and if they have been a redshirt they have to do that again to play their fifth year.

By then the athlete ought to have his degree. And, if not, there is the opportunity for post-eligibility assistance.

Those progress rules are more stringent rules than apply to the non-athlete in the general student population.

I think all schools are graduating many more players now that we've got the rule that requires athletes to declare a major after two years. Before that rule was passed, athletes would bounce around from department to department, taking all the easy courses they could find. They'd stay eligible for five years without ever declaring a major. As a result, they would still be two years away from a degree when their eligibility was used up. That's one of the reasons why the graduation rate was not as good as it should have been.

Then there is Proposition 48, the requirement that an incoming athlete has passed a certain number of hours of math, sciences, English and other "core" college prep subjects in order to be eligible to participate. They must also receive a required score on their college board exams. As a result we're getting better students.

I am realistic enough to know that there are always going to be a few seniors each year on our team who are just hanging on to play football to see if they can make it in the NFL. But even some of those athletes have come back after a few years to finish up and get their degree.

Our biggest hope, with the increased entrance requirements from Prop 48, that the high schools will hold up their end of that bargain by better preparing young men and women for college level work. As of now, some are. Some aren't.

It's easy to sit and be critical, but I think the ones who are not doing a very good job are some of the innercity schools that don't have the necessary funds. Because of lack of dollars, they don't have the number of coaches needed to do the counseling and get the players into the correct courses and see that they buckle down and work on their studies so they will be eligible to accept a college scholarship.

You feel sorry for the staffs at schools like that as they struggle to help their students survive. They don't have the money for the education. They don't pay the teachers well enough. They don't have the books or supplies. Those kids who need it the most are the ones who are getting shortchanged.

It's unfortunate, but there are many high school athletes who could qualify athletically to play at the major college level who don't have the core courses or don't get the required minimum test score.

But it's not all the fault of the teachers and coaches. We are offering an opportunity for those young people, but they have to do the work.

There is another thing we get into as coaches. Many of these youngsters don't have anyone in their entire family who has ever gone to college. And they didn't plan to go. But by the time they are juniors in high school they start to develop and blossom as a great player. Now the youngster is told he's good enough to earn a college athletic scholarship.

The problem is, even at that time, it could easily be too late for him to get into all the right core courses that he would need to make him eligible to accept a scholarship and for admission.

The good solid high school programs, where they continually are putting a lot of students and athletes into college each year, the coaches are counseling the ninth graders, making sure they get into the right courses from the start.

And those kids are motivated because they have seen other athletes go on to college and they have role models to look up to.

Hopefully, these changes will result in more media stories about the valuable college education being received by young men who wouldn't have ever gotten to college were it not for athletics.

Dealing with the media is not always the most pleasant task, although I have had a very good relationship with the vast majority of the people who have covered our team over the years.

A few years back I had a problem over a long established policy of mine which has ever since affected the way the media covers our practices.

We have basically always had a policy of closed practices. We let pro scouts in to watch and we have always let in anyone we can vouch for who is close to the program, like alumni, boosters, students or faculty.

And we allowed the media in, but I had an agreement with them that they were not to ever print anything that would affect the game plan. In other words, they could not put anything in the paper about a position move I might make that would give away what our plans were going to be, or our schemes. Any subtle change I might make, I didn't want to read about that in the paper.

After all, I didn't want the opponent to know about such things until they saw them in the game. So strategy and injuries were on my "no no" list.

Here's what I asked of the media as far as injuries were concerned. I wasn't going to be dishonest. But, if an injury occurred in practice, I wanted 24 hours before it became public. I wanted overnight. I wanted the

After quarterback Gary Conklin hurt his thumb in practice, the media coverage rules were changed.

player to get his treatment started, come back in the morning and see the doctor. Then we could make an intelligent decision about whether or not he could play.

If the player was hurt but was going to be okay to play the following Saturday, I didn't want the injury mentioned. I didn't want the opponent to read that his left knee is bruised or his right ankle is sore. There are pileups in the sport of football and things have happened where a player's known injury has been attacked.

If a player gets hurt in a game and everybody knows he is hurt, but we aren't going to know his status for sure until the following Wednesday, I'll say that and then tell you on Wednesday what the medical decision is.

Quite often, a player can appear to be hurt rather seriously in a practice and is taken off the field. Yet, after some treatment and rest, he may be ready to go again by morning. As far as I'm concerned, that just doesn't need to be written about at all.

This one time, when we were getting ready to play USC, quarterback Cary Conklin suffered a thumb injury in practice.

Of course the media guys were all out there and saw him go into the training room. After practice I told them, "Nothing has changed. I don't want to read about this in the paper. If we get word tomorrow that Cary can't play, then we'll get another quarterback ready and I'll tell you."

Well, in this one case, one of the writers blew the whistle on the Conklin injury, released the story and thus didn't respect my policy.

It just infuriated me that, after all the years of being as outgoing and honest as I could possibly be with the media, that this would happen. So, I closed them out and thus ended the opportunity for any of them to attend practice.

Most all of the media people ganged up on me for a while. That was all right. I can handle it. But it's so much better now, not having them at our daily in-season workouts.

I let the media in during spring practice and also during fall camp. But once the season starts, that's it.

Even when they were allowed in, I held a press conference after practice to answer any questions they might have. I do the same now. Nothing has really changed except they just haven't seen the practice. So, they ask their questions and I give them my answers.

I continue to be as cooperative as I can. Sometimes, if we've got an internal problem or a player has a problem that the media people have heard a rumor about, I may ask for some temporary protection until the true facts are known. But then I'll level with the media on just about anything. I will not however explain why a particular player has been disciplined if the situation is not public. The athletes deserve some privacy.

Unlike the problems encountered by some pro teams, female sportswriters in the locker room has not been a problem for me because a policy was in place before I arrived.

Up until a year before I was hired, the press would come into the dressing room after a game to interview the players. When the first female writer showed up they decided the fair thing was to bar everyone.

From then on, and we still adhere to that policy, we bring the players requested by the writers to a special interview room away from where the players are showering and dressing.

If I coached for another 100 years you could never convince me that a woman should be permitted in a man's locker room or men should be allowed in a woman's dressing room regardless of the reason.

chapter thirty three

*People wonder what
the future holds for me.
Retirement? A new job?*

I have not given retirement much thought. Obviously I cannot pinpoint a day or time for that to happen. I'm afraid that if a coach seriously entertained such a thought he would subconsciously stop recruiting.

It seems to be an accepted fact that a young coach is going to get fired and an older one is headed to another school, the NFL or is going to retire. And any of those rumors will be quickly used against you in recruiting.

I don't have any set time frame as to the length of time I will continue to coach. I have a four-year contract. But, if we had continued to play the way we played in 1988, and if the spiral had continued downward, I probably would have been "retired" by now. And maybe not by my own choice.

There are great challenges in this job. The challenge of putting a staff together. Of putting the team together. And then the challenge of 11 or 12 games a year — breaking down the opponent, the scouting report, devising a game plan and then going out to orchestrate the contest.

And that challenge is just as exciting to me today as it's ever been. That's why I'm a coach. I not only enjoy it but it's what I always wanted to do — teach and be with young men and make them better. Take them as far as they can go in their sport. Try to lead by example.

There are still a lot of goals for me to achieve. I think that the goal of becoming the conference champion at any time in your career is an enjoyable, difficult, and satisfying accomplishment. Plus there is always that elusive goal of becoming the national champion.

When I talk about a national championship, I'm not talking about gaining such an honor for me as the coach. I've had plenty of honors — Coach of the Year and becoming the winningest coach in Pac-10 history. I'm talking about the fantastic thrill it would be to reach that ultimate goal for a group of our kids and for our university. And I just know that we won't have a chance to reach that goal unless we are team oriented.

If we're out there worrying about how many catches some receiver is going to get or how many yards a running back is going to gain, we're not going to make it as a team. Yet I'm not opposed, as we get toward the end of a season, of helping a player get some individual recognition. If we've got the game on ice and Greg Lewis has 98 yards, I'm going to put him in and let him get to 100 because that's the magic number. But I'm not going to leave a quarterback in to throw for 400 or 500 yards. I want to get the young back-up players in the game.

Once the season starts, I won't let anybody talk publicly to the press about bowls. I don't like to either. But in our own team meetings, it's important for the players to be aware of where we are in the polls and where we can get to if we win the next game. If that will help the motivation, why not. That's just another chip on the table. And I won't hesitate to use it.

I don't like to talk a lot about the Rose Bowl to the team. But everyone needs intermediate and long range goals. Some people think it's a jinx to look ahead. Not me. I think it's important to be aware of what lies in the future.

Take this coming schedule in 1991. I realize the game will have been played by the time this book comes out, but when you look at the conference schedule you see Stanford on the road. That is going to be a tough game and the team that wins that game will stay in the league race for another five weeks for sure.

Then, when you look at the non-conference schedule and see a team like Nebraska on there, you've got to be dumb not to know that's the kind of game that could get you in a January 1 bowl if you miss the conference championship. We can't afford to overlook anyone before that game. But when that time arrives, you just add up the things that can give your team extra motivation.

The real fun of coaching is walking into a victorious locker room. You can't believe the thrills we had in our locker room this past season. The players and coaches have all devoted hours and hours in preparation. You live with the heartaches, the pain and fatigue. But when you win there is just no better feeling. People who haven't experienced that feeling just can't understand it.

On the other side of the coin, the emotion, the agony that you feel after a bitter and crushing defeat can also only be experienced in a locker room. You've gone so far and you're oh so close. Then a loss. It creates an incredible amount of pain. The lessons learned though can be so valuable for our young men.

If there is a depressing side to coaching it comes from fans who go to a pre-game luncheon, have several drinks, then go and watch the game, second guess, boo

Contemplating the future . . . Reflecting on the past . . .
Or planning how to beat the next opponent?

and criticize, then go home thinking they have all of the answers and are so judgmental.

Unless they've been in the arena, they don't understand what these kids go through. That's why it hurts so much when you see or hear criticism of the athlete. Especially the amateur athlete.

Husky football for years was the big show in town. As a result, the university had its base established before the others came along. The second thing is that when pro football came to town we took the approach of working together. The Nordstroms, the original owners of the Seahawks, are not only University of Washington alums but continue to be fans and supporters of the Huskies.

We've tried to work in consort with the Seahawks. And so have they. The two organizations have tried to help each other and not have any kind of an adversarial relationship.

The other pro sport teams have also been very supportive. The Sonics have helped UW basketball and the Mariners have helped UW baseball. I don't think it's been a problem from that standpoint. I think the obvious problem we all have is that there is a limit to how many recreational dollars are available to be spent. That makes the bottom line for all of us two words — don't lose.

That's the key. Our 1988 team was very competitive. But we lost five games and there were a lot of disgruntled fans — even if the five losses were by a total of just 15 points. And season tickets fell off.

The key thing, now that we have an established winning program, is to maintain it. In a lean year we aren't going to fill a 73,000-seat stadium, but our base is such now that I would think we could keep the crowds at least in the 50s. We've sold on the average about 60,000 season tickets each of the last few years.

I really can't imagine coaching anywhere but here at Washington. I've had other offers during the years.

And I've had an opportunity to interview for other college jobs on two or three different occasions, but I haven't taken them.

The one exception, I suppose, was the Ohio State job when they were after a replacement for Woody Hayes. That was the strangest situation I ever went through.

One day I got a call from Hugh Hindman, the athletic director at Ohio State. He said, "We've completed our search now and have it down to three coaches. And you are one of them."

I said, "What?" I'd had absolutely zero contact with them. No phone calls, no letters, no nothing, no interest.

I told Hugh I was very happy at Washington and wasn't looking for a different job. I was about to leave for Japan to coach in the Japan Bowl for the first time.

Hugh said the complete Ohio State search committee would be in San Francisco and asked if I wouldn't at least talk to them. He again said that they were down to three coaches and that I was one of them.

I met with them briefly before taking off for Tokyo. I didn't seek the job. And it wasn't offered to me. I'm not sure I would have had enough courage to turn it down. A headline reading 'Massillon Boy Returns Home' would have had a lot of appeal, at least in Ohio.

But I had also read Woody Hayes' book, '100-yard War'. I remember when I finished reading it I mentioned to Carol, "That's one school where I'd never want to coach." Woody talked about the tremendous pressure that exists there. There is pressure in coaching anywhere. But more some places than others.

Many coaches, after a long career, seem to look at becoming their school's athletic director. I made up my mind some time ago that I don't want to be an athletic director.

An athletic director is a fund raiser, a counselor, and an advisor. They are hiring — and firing — people all the time. Our department is incredibly large and difficult to manage. And you've got to deal with administration, the NCAA, the President's Commission, the students and the faculty, and committees of all kinds. And you've got a lot of people out there trying to tell you how to do your job and a large number who think they know how to run an athletic department.

I've got enough of those already. They're up in the stands.